How to Date a Younger Man

The Cougar's Guide to Cubhunting

Kate Mulvey

CARLTON
BOOKS

Contents

Introduction

Ladies, you are about to embark on a journey that could change your life. More than just a book, this is a manifesto packed full of advice and tips that aim to unleash your true fantastic self and empower you to go out there and get any man you want. The message I want to give you in this book is simply that you are an amazing woman, and who can do and get what you want out of life.

Times have changed since women got married in their twenties, popped out a couple of kids, hit middle age and retired silently into the background, while their men ran off with the 21-year-old secretary. Fast forward to the twenty-first century and, believe me, it is a cougar world. Women don't put up with being the "second sex" anymore, and one way that we are enjoying ourselves is by embracing the older woman/younger man relationship. Whether it is for a bit of fun between the sheets, a way to boost our middle-age ego, or love actually, dating a younger man is fast becoming a growing trend.

And why not? On planet celebrity, dating down the age scale is all the rage. If Madonna, Cher, Halle, et al, can do it, then so can you. After all, there are so many younger men out there who are just waiting for a hot mama like you to come along. And we are hot. Age is no longer a barrier to being sexy. For the forty-something gals, who work at it, you can easily have a bodylicious sex appeal well into your late fifties. All it takes is care, attention and some good old-fashioned pride in who you are.

There is a whole gaggle of great women out there, either divorced or single, who have done the life of cooking dinner, standing by their man and sacrificing themselves to the needs and wants of others. And besides, they have probably been welded to the Rampant Rabbit for the last few months rather than a flesh-and-blood man. Good-looking, full of life, the forty-something woman is now looking for fun, companionship and a great sex life. Only this time with a sweet young guy who will adore her and make love to her all night.

So if you want to try your hand at dating younger men, then, this is the manual for you. Throughout the next ten chapters, you will learn what it is to be a cougar, how to unleash your inner confidence and how get rid of the fears that hold you back. Full of fun, insightful quizzes such as "What Cougar Are You?" and "What Is Your Sexual Style?", to name but a few, here's a book that is fun and entertaining. Packed with tips on how to prepare yourself for the hunt, how to charm your way to the first date, what to say and how to dress, there is also information on where to find your cute cub, advice on how to get round toy-boy talk, how to bridge the generational age gap and ways to make your relationship stay the course. This guide will teach you what to expect in the toy-boy dating world – the pitfalls, the pleasures and some of the situations you might find yourself in.

By the end of the book, you will have learned the means and techniques to stay in control of the dating game, and achieved the glow that only inner confidence can give. So much so, that you will vastly increase your chances of dating a younger man. It doesn't mean you have to abandon the older man altogether, it just means that with so many more choices in the dating pool, you will never have to spend a night alone, unless you want to.

So enjoy the ride. Because, here's the thing: There are no guarantees in life, so why not live life for the moment? Go cougar!

"The difference between a successful person and others is not a lack

of strength, not a lack of knowledge, but rather a lack of will."

Vince Lombardi

1

The Cougar: Who Is She?

"When I'm good, I'm very good.

When I'm bad, I'm better."

Mae West

There's a creature prowling around the urban landscape –
the cougar. So who is this latest addition to the block? She
is a new breed of single, older woman in her 30s, 40s (or
so), who goes hotly in pursuit of younger men. Confident,
sassy and sexy, she knows exactly what she wants. What she
wants is a cub (a cute guy at least eight years her junior).
What she doesn't need is a man with a belly, wispy hair,
baggage and a mid-life crisis. Ditto: Kids, cohabitation or
commitment. The lady wants to play!

"For every stunning, smart, well-coiffed hot woman of 40-plus there is a balding, paunchy relic in yellow pants making a fool of himself with some 22-year-old waitress. Ladies, I apologize." *Andy Rooney*

In fact, the cougar is simply doing what men have done throughout history: If they can trot around town with girls half their age and society doesn't bat an eyelid then it's surely time for the cougar to gallivant about in tight dresses and hunt down some tender meat of her own. Divorced or newly single, she may have a husband (or two) in the background plus the accompanying spoils of a marriage (or two), a brilliant career and a thirst for carousing and generally having a good time. Who knows, she may be too busy climbing the career ladder for a full-on relationship with a man her own age. Or maybe she's had her heart broken too many times and all she wants now is a sweet younger man to put a smile on her face.

The Cougar Craze

Cougars seem to be the latest trend sweeping Hollywood (and the rest of the world), with celebrity women flying the cougar flag and showing off their arm candy at premieres, after-parties and on the red carpet. Let's take a look at some of them.

Queen of the Cougars Demi Moore ensured permanent paparazzi attention for herself following her marriage to fellow actor Ashton Kutcher, who is 15 years younger. When he posted a picture of her naked butt on Twitter, she just laughed! Cougars take these things in their stride.

Material Girl Madonna is destined never to give up the hunt. Her one-time personal trainer and now devoted father to her daughter Lourdes, Carlos Leon, is eight years younger than her. Even ex-hubbie Guy Ritchie is 10 years her junior. He now has a new partner – Jacqui Ainsley – a younger, fresher version of Madge, with less attitude and a sweeter smile. Not that Madonna would care: she moved on well before Ritchie bagged his babe and got herself a Brazilian model: Jesus Luz, 23. She may have moved on from her baby-model, but no doubt now the diva has tasted such tender flesh, she will be going back for more.

Then there's the Brit filmmaker, photographer and conceptual artist Sam Taylor-Wood, who has not only given birth to Wylda Rae at 43, but is also engaged to her cub: Aaron Johnson, 19. With her tiny, yoga-trained frame, she reveals that he is the mature one in the relationship: "He's more mature now than are a lot of men my age. He stops me from spinning out and being a complete nutter, which I'm definitely capable of. He grounds me and keeps me calmer." Taylor-Wood has had her own traumas: she was twice diagnosed with cancer but managed to battle her way through it. Not only this but she valiantly refused any of husband Jay Joplin's money when they divorced amicably in September 2008. This one really does seem like a love story.

And your average woman is catching on fast. Recently, a study by online dating service www.parship.co.uk revealed that 280,000 British women over the age of 45 are keen to date a younger man, a leap of 20 per cent in a year! In America, the craze is skyrocketing, with whole websites such as www.gocougar.com and www.toyboywarehouse.com dedicated to hooking up twenty-something men with women in their 40s (or older).

"The older theory was, marry an older man because they're more mature.

But the new theory is men don't mature. Marry a younger one."

Rita Rudner

Embrace the Cougar Lifestyle

At some stage in life most women will go through a cougar phase. When it's your turn, enjoy, even though there will always be some people in society who might look down on you for dating younger men. For all the strides women have made over the years, the old dating double standard still exists. Older men feel discarded, which makes them feel threatened, insecure and out to put you down. And older women who are not cougars are no help either. Stuck in a marriage or dating an old codger, they are simply jealous of all the fun and sex you are getting. But if you don't care, what does it matter? Whether it leads to a permanent liaison or simply kick-starts your confidence, the cougar lifestyle can be a truly liberating choice. So have you got what it takes?

The Cougar Checklist

Above all, today's cougar …

… Is not needy. She has her own financial security, most probably gained via an established career. What's more, she values her freedom and friendships and is at a time in her life when she enjoys doing what she wants, when she wants (and often that means a young cub).

… Is dynamic. Full of vitality, a cougar is the kind of woman who has a life crammed full of activities (she probably goes scuba diving or kickboxing before breakfast!).

… Looks younger than her age. She may be the older woman but she sure knows how to keep herself young! The cougar defies the ageing process. Well, they say 40 is the new 30 and this particular woman knows how to present her personal best.

... Is comfortable with her own sexuality, even if she's a bit on the craggy side (she doesn't care two hoots about crows' feet – she'll probably have them zapped, anyway). And if her derrière is heading south, she'll either go to the gym and/or wear magic underwear.

... Knows herself and doesn't care what anyone else thinks. A cougar is guilt-free: she has absolutely no intention of hiding her predatory ways. Indeed, she's a roaring success. Above all, she is proud that she can pull a younger guy in the face of stiff competition.

... Is independent. Cougars are comfortable being alone. They've spent time in and out of relationships and consequently, they know how to get along without a man and they don't need a boyfriend attached to their side to be happy. This means the cougar is less likely to be clingy or needy – which let's face it, men don't find very attractive. Besides, a cougar has got her life pretty much sorted. She has lots of friends (people love to be around a sexy, confident woman). And when she's not roaring about town at lunches or cocktail parties, she can kick back, crack open a bottle and pamper herself in her beautiful house. Cosy and content in her pastel pashmina, she'll be watching an old movie or reading her favourite book.

... Is assertive. A cougar has a clear sense of who she is, and what she wants. Therefore she's less timid when it comes to men.

... Is in her sexual prime. At 40, women are at their peak whereas men are in their prime at 18 and keep going strong at least until their mid-30s. Cougars are old enough to enjoy a young man's enthusiastic charms. And if he's lucky maybe she can teach him a thing or two. After all, the cougar knows all about the benefits of good sex.

And finally... A true cougar is a realist. Sooner than later, her cub may leave and she understands that. So for now, she'll enjoy him for his sex drive and all the attention she can get. With their baby faces, some younger guys are refreshingly sweet and full of youthful hope and joy, which can be catching. Often that's quite enough to reignite the cougar's flame for fun and she'll move on in search of fresher meat.

"A hard man is good to find." *Mae West*

What a Cougar *Will* Do ...

✴ Give the best blow jobs – after all, she's been in training for years.

✴ Almost always pay for the date.

✴ Have a drawer full of sex toys and condoms, oils and fruit-flavoured lubes.

✴ Wear the sexiest lingerie. Whether it's black lacy stockings and bra or crotchless panties, she knows how to flaunt her assets.

✴ Understand the male mind – most probably, she has a son (or nephew) the same age.

✴ Drink beer out of a bottle and knock back the Tequila shots.

✴ Have phone sex and send sexy texts (complete with picture).

✴ Flatly refuse to pass her amuse-by date.

✴ Have a good time – fun is top of the cougar agenda!

What a Cougar *Won't* Do ...

* Date an older man or even one her own age – she's been there and got the granddad vest!

* Give her cub a hard time if he's late (all the better to scan the bar for alternative prey).

* Wear orthopaedic footwear – stilettos or barefoot, purrlease!

* Sink into a poor-me-pity slump – she's far too busy hunting.

* Cry if her boy tells her she looks fat.

* Or wake him up in the middle of the night to ask if he loves her.

A Cougar *Will* Say ...

"Make mine a big one, and that's not just my Martini!"

"Where's the party?"

"No, they are *not* real!"

But She'll *Never* Say ...

"Do you love me?"

"Where is this relationship going?"

or even ...

"Not tonight, I've got a headache!"

Cougar Do's and Don'ts

Don't get drunk on the hunt. Really, there's no dignity in being slumped on a chair, with your dress round your armpits when you're over 40. If you must down the shots, wait till you get him back to your lair.

Do insist he wears a condom. He may be young, but that doesn't mean he hasn't been round the block! Catch a rash and you'll scratching your way around town instead of purring.

Don't go for a virgin. On second thoughts, if you really must … After all, it's been a long-established practice for a young cub to be initiated by a more experienced older woman: think Mrs Robinson!

Do discover your USP if you haven't already. We all have something about us that's unique so find yours and use it to your advantage.

Don't whine or complain, leave that to the younger cats!

Do show him off to your friends (especially your ex). There's nothing like young arm candy to say, "I'm back in demand, so watch out!"

Don't agree to meet his mom unless you really have to (impending marriage). She may be younger than you, you'll probably be hotter/slimmer and she'll do her utmost best to protect her cub at all costs.

Do snog him and have fun dancing with him at a party. What better way to make your fellow cougars jealous?

"Some of us are becoming the men we wanted to marry."

Gloria Steinem

Cougar Style

Empowered women (aka iconic cougars) have been dating the younger man since Neanderthal woman dragged young Ug back to her cave to chomp on a bison sandwich. Whether she is the controlling Alpha Cougar, an attention-seeking Goddess Cougar, the more serious Careful Cougar, or the gentle Cougar Lite, each woman has her own style. So what's yours?

Controlling Alpha Cougar – Mrs Robinson in *The Graduate*

The #1 celluloid cougar Mrs Robinson (aka Anne Bancroft, the middle-aged woman stuck in a loveless marriage) has an affair with the virgin son of her husband's business partner. This über cougar calls all the shots, telling poor Benjamin Braddock when and where to meet, and generally marshalling his every move. Whatever the outcome, there's no debate that she's the all-time greatest movie cougar.

Goddess Cougar – Mae West

She looked like a sex siren and ate men alive! Actress and ultimate attention-seeking cougar Mae West was known for her numerous sexual conquests, even when she was married. At 61, she became romantically involved with Chester Rybonski, one of the musclemen in her Las Vegas stage show. He was 30 years younger than West.

Careful Cougar – Susan Sarandon

Steady and reasonable, she has always maintained a kind of equality in relationships with her cubs. Her first big catch was Italian director Franco Amurri in the mid-1980s when she was around 40, while he was closer to 28. When she met her next cub, Tim Robbins (11 years younger) on the set of *Bull Durham* in 1988, it was the start of a long liaison.

Cougar Lite – Elizabeth Taylor

Liz finally went for cougar bait in 1991 when she wed twice-married construction worker Larry Fortensky, whom she met at the Betty Ford Center in 1988. They were married when she was 59 and he was just 39. Even though she was 20 years older than him, she always let him "be the man".

Know Your Cougar Style

While all cougars share the same core values, like the siblings in one same family, often they differ in style and characteristics. Complete our quiz to see how you score!

1 How would you rate your dress sense?
   a) Sexy, smart and always sharp.
   b) Fashionable with a twist.
   c) Understated and classic.
   d) Comfortable, free-flowing and feminine.

2 You are at a party. Do you …
   a) Stand at the doorway and scan the room for the best-looking cub before making a beeline for him.
   b) Have fun and flirt with all the young men there before dancing the night away.
   c) Check out the young prey and chose your victim with care.
   d) Hang about the edges of the party, smiling prettily and hoping one of the younger men will approach you.

3 Which of these sums up your motto?
   a) Success is all.
   b) Live life with a passion.
   c) Balance in life is key.
   d) I just want to be happy.

4 How do you feel about mind games?
   a) Whatever it takes to get to the goal is fine by me.
   b) I have a personality that needs them.
   c) Mind games can blow up in your face so I tend to steer clear of them.
   d) Why play mind games? I want to be liked!

5 Which of these irritates you most?

a) Inefficiency and indecision – why can't everyone be like me?

b) Narrow-mindedness and inflexibility.

c) Surprises – I like to know what I'm getting!

d) Insensitivity and impatience.

6 What do you fear most?

a) Loss of control.

b) Being lonely.

c) Social embarrassment.

d) Confrontation.

7 What do you want most?

a) To be in charge.

b) Admired.

c) Correct.

d) Liked.

8 Where would you prefer to take your cub on holiday?

a) Somewhere I know really well so I can take charge.

b) A place that will be an adventure for us both.

c) To my usual holiday destination, where I feel safe.

d) I always let him choose.

9 So, how do you treat your cub?

a) I like to focus my attention on him – and know where he is at all times.

b) I'm witty and fun company, always.

c) Even though he's only 20, I still want a mutual adult connection.

d) I want to make him feel loved, warm and safe.

10 Time to get naked with your cub! Do you …

a) Blindfold him before the surprise.

b) Do the Dance of the Seven Veils, complete with costume.

c) Make sure you look your best, with low lighting and a sexy negligée.

d) Turn off the lights and crawl under the sheets.

Mostly As
Alpha Cougar
The most powerful of the cougars, the AC is bound to score more cubs at any feeding frenzy. Fast and strategic, she always does what it takes to get what she wants – which is usually her own way. But her competitive spirit plus the need to always be in control often masks an insecure animal. Be careful or your cub might find you too overwhelming. Try to be more easy-going and let him chose the restaurant sometimes.

Mostly Bs
Goddess Cougar
The most brilliant of all the cougars, you're also the most fashionable. Intense and emotional, you are a feeling animal and you just love to party. Cubs enjoy being around you as you bubble over with warmth and fun. Impulsive and dramatic, you can tire easily of your cub if he does not meet your stimulation-meter. Go easy: he's young and he might not be as confident as you are. Under attack, you may resort to biting sarcasm.

Mostly Cs
Careful Cougar
Steady and correct, you are the most stable of the wild cats and also the most rational. More conservative in your appearance and habits, your hunting style is organized and strategic: you proceed with caution. The most tenacious of all the cougars, you will work tirelessly if there's a cub you want to get your claws into. At times you might be seen as cold and distant, so be careful: your cub will not be sophisticated enough to read between the lines.

Mostly Ds
Cougar Lite
Highly domesticated, Cougar Lite (CL) is so tame that she's the least cougar-like of the cougars! This one hunts at a slow and easy pace and is friendly to her quarry. She gains security through close relationships and once with her cub, she tends to submit to him. Pleasant and non-competitive, she will support and encourage him. She hates confrontation but she's not to be underestimated: she has a strong sense of values and if she is messed around, there's no turning back. Caution: keep him entertained or he may get bored. You will appeal to a cub in search of a mommy cougar.

Cougar Glossary

Read our short guide of what to look out for on Planet Cougar.

An old soul: A younger person, who was born mature.

Cougar: Woman, 40 years of age or older, who pursues younger men typically more than eight years her junior.

Cradle robber or cradle snatcher: A person who is involved with a much younger individual.

Cub: Younger male who is going out with an older partner, often paired with the term **Cougar**.

Leopard: A cougar over the age 50-mark, who has gained her age spots!

May–December romance: A relationship in which the age difference between the two adults is wide enough to risk social disapproval.

MILF: Acronym of Mother I'd Like (Love) to F***; a sexually desirable older woman, not necessarily one who has kids.

Puma: Woman in her late 20s or 30s who dates a younger man (i.e. a twenty-something) and is often considered a "cougar in training". Term can also apply to a cougar whose age disparity is less than eight years.

Sugar Daddy/Mama/Mommy: A rich (and usually older) person who offers money or gifts to a less wealthy, usually younger person in return for companionship and/or sexual favours.

Toy Boy/Boy Toy: A much younger boyfriend.

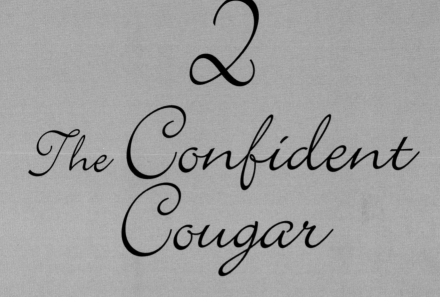

2
The Confident Cougar

"Sex appeal is 50 per cent what you've got, and
50 per cent what people think you've got."
Sophia Loren

To succeed with your cub, confidence is the key word – it's
what marks out the cougar from the kitten. All cougars
know that feeling good on the inside is more attractive
than all the face creams you can slather on yourself, or the
sparkly halterneck dresses you might buy. We all want that
"I look-so-great-I-fancy-myself" feeling – in short, the
magical radiance that lights up whenever we are feeling
good about ourselves.

How to Be Cougar-tastic (Or The Inner Cougar)

In an ideal world, we would all be confident cougars, getting our claws out at the whiff of tender flesh, but of course everyone has times when they feel like a wet rag or perhaps you're just having a bad day. Daily attacks are negative thoughts, however and nagging concerns like "Why, oh why can't I find a man? Aargh!" or even "I'm going to starve myself to get to a size 0" can chip away at your self-confidence if you're not careful. The good news is it all comes down to how you feel, so learn to love yourself.

Must get slimmer/brainier/wittier … it's a real challenge, being cougar-tastic! So often we set ourselves unrealistic standards to live up to, and if we don't meet those exacting benchmarks (and most of us, admittedly, do not), our self-confidence slowly goes into decline. We need to accept ourselves and be happy with who we are. Getting out your inner cougar is all about being your own personal best so don't go comparing yourself to the "Perfect Slebs" – Angelina, Jennifer or J Lo. There's always going to be someone younger/prettier/richer than you, but who cares?

"Sometimes courage doesn't always roar. Sometimes courage is the quiet voice at the end of the day, saying, 'I will try again tomorrow.'" *Mary Anne Radmacher*

Learn Cougar Confidence

According to psychologists, approximately 8 out of 10 women are thought to suffer a lack of self-confidence, compared to just 5 in 10 men. Women, it seems, have to ward off more attacks on their self-esteem on a daily basis. Help! These quick confidence boosters will soon pull you out of the negative thought trap.

Take a break. It's hard to boost confidence levels if you're feeling anxious or nervous. One way to beat those nerves is to learn some relaxation techniques, so try this five-minute exercise. Sit on a chair with your right hand hanging down by your side, your left hand resting on your thigh. Now close your eyes and slowly breathe in for a count of six, hold for a count of two and then breathe out for four. Breathe deeply, concentrating on the blood flowing from your heart and down your right arm. Imagine it reaching your fingertips, going back up your arm and continuing round your body. Keep breathing slowly.

Straighten up. A recent study from the University of Ohio found that the simple act of sitting up straight and significantly adjusting your posture boosts confidence. So try this simple trick the next time you are sitting at a bar and watch the results! And it makes you look taller and slimmer, too.

Break a sweat. If you're feeling low, go for a walk around the block. The simple act of exercise (it doesn't matter how long, how intense or how often) gives an instant body image boost and gets those feel-good hormones racing round your body. Men love it when a woman has a healthy glow and you might find yourself attracting attention, which can bring a smile to any woman's face. Try it at least three times a week and you'll start to notice little changes in your body that you will like.

Get a new look. Whether it's a dramatic new haircut or dyeing your hair strawberry blonde, buying more daring clothes or even a luscious lipstick, a makeover is a quick way to feel better about yourself. Changing your look or just indulging in a little "me" time can up your self-esteem in a big way.

Have a home spa. A spot of pampering makes you feel special and you'll also feel good about yourself. When you're home alone, run a bubble bath, put on your favourite music and pour yourself a cocktail. You deserve it!

Be kind. If you want to build up your confidence in a big way, do something nice once a week. It may seem strange, but the thanks you receive immediately reinforces your self-worth, so volunteer to help some kids, deliver meals on wheels or just compliment a friend – it will make you feel better about yourself.

Make a list. Avoiding things that are stressing you out increases anxiety and cuts down confidence. Write down anything that may fall into this category, such as calling people back or paying bills. Start off by tackling just two things – and do them today!

Set a (small) goal. One of the most effective ways to build self-confidence is to break down large goals into small, do-able action steps. For example, if you're trying to shape up and get into your sexy dress, make it a goal to eat at least three daily servings of vegetables or salad.

Try something new. It may seem daunting, even scary, but tackling something new increases your sense of wellbeing. Here are a few suggestions to get you started: learn a new language, try designing your own clothes, take up the Tango or belly dancing (great for the stomach) or register for car maintenance at a local community college (all those hot young boys!).

Seek reassurance. Sometimes we need a little boost from another, so ask someone close to you for reassurance. Those kind and encouraging words can make all the difference. Don't be afraid to go to your loved ones whenever you need a little extra help!

Get a good night's sleep. Make sure you don't ditch the zzzzzzs! It's a known fact that a lack of sleep makes you feel less confident, tetchy and less able to weather the daily knocks. Make the bedroom cool and calm, listen to some relaxing music or read a book and sip a herbal tea before you drop off to sleep. Even missing an hour of shut eye can play havoc with our skin and age us according to surveys carried out by the UK's Sleep Council.

"The road to success is always under construction."

Lily Tomlin

Cougar-tastic Body Language Secrets

Looking more confident opens you up to more encounters with likely toy-boy prey. Just follow the quick tips on our cheat sheet!

Don't slouch – at best, you'll look tired but you might also resemble a juvenile delinquent. Stand tall: straighten your back and pull your shoulders back. Not only will this make you look like a fearless feline, but by letting the oxygen into your lungs, you will feel energized and more confident.

Do hold your head high, possibly tilted backward (not too far or you might get dizzy!). This will give you the appearance of being in control.

Don't cross your arms. It just says, "Help! I feel shy and nervous," or even, "Back off, big boy!" If you find yourself crossing your arms, get some props: holding a drink in one hand will make you feel more at ease. Be careful you don't down too much alcohol or else you might find yourself toppling over, though!

Do lock eyes with other cougars (and anyone else in the room). This says, "I belong here and I'm proud". But do tilt your head, too – it is a sign of friendliness and softness, great to follow if you've just been locking a gaze with someone. Go, cougar!

Don't fiddle with your hair or your earrings – it will make you look unsure of yourself. Hunching your shoulders and hanging your head is a mark of low self-confidence, too.

Don't swagger – it looks as if you're trying too hard. Even if she doesn't always feel like it inside, a cougar appears cool and self-assured at all times, not desperate to prove herself.

Do smile from the heart. Maybe this one sounds obvious but smiling with cold (cod fish) eyes is bound to turn people off rather than on. Think of someone you really like – a small child always gives us warm feelings – and let that feeling flood over you till your mouth naturally feels itself smiling. It works every time.

"I shall stay the way I am, because I do not give a damn."

Dorothy Parker

Be a Big Cat in the Jungle

Did you know that successful people spend only 10 per cent of their time dwelling on problems and 90 per cent thinking up a solution? Our special formula contains all the secrets to being a fearless feline!

Ditch the doubt. It might seem impossible to be a confident cougar if all you're feeling is that you want to climb under the duvet and eat ice-cream, so stand in front of the mirror and try positive affirmations. Repeating positive phrases such as "I am successful" or "I'm worth it", just like the advert, can make a huge difference to a person's self-esteem. It might not seem like much but the more you repeat these upbeat mantras, the more likely you are to start believing them.

Step outside your comfort zone. OK, it may be nice and easy to do the same things and see the same people but getting stuck in a comfort rut will hold you back from being a fearless feline. Not only that but how are you going to meet all those toy boys if you're stuck at home? Try a new thing every day: accept that invitation to a cool new gallery opening or a party where you won't know everyone or take a different route to work. Breaking with your usual routine also breaks the comfort cycle.

Welcome the worst. OK, so you got a bit drunk, knocked the drinks over and your tights were ripped on a spiky bush. But was it really so bad? Trying to imagine the worst thing that can happen when you go somewhere new calms you down. The fear will run away, the more you chase it.

Visualize your fear. If welcoming the worst just got you into a total panic fest, try this instead. Take a moment to close your eyes and imagine a place of safety and calm: it could be a picture of you walking on a beautiful beach or snuggled up in bed with your cub saying sweet things to you. Let those positive feelings flood over you until you start to feel more relaxed.

Bounce back. Any fearless feline develops an inner resilience – she knows setbacks and rejections are a part of life. So, it's stressful, but remember the only time when you're not feeling some degree of stress is when you're 10 feet underground! So, if that first date ends without a kiss, a phone number or even a goodbye, who cares? Make a promise not to dwell on it and swiftly move onto to the next.

Think big. Every fearless feline knows the key to getting what she wants is effort, planning and good old-fashioned hard work. One habit will get you ahead of the pack: start thinking big. The difference between success and failure is that often the successful person thinks they deserve it: high achievers have faith in themselves. So, you might not start out feeling that way but this is something that can be learned. Also, if you believe in yourself, others will.

"I succeeded by saying what everyone else was thinking."

Joan Rivers

Wake Up the Sexy Cat Inside You!

Fearless Felines ...

* Like to drive fast in open-top cars.

* Learn from their mistakes and grab whatever chances life throws at them.

* Are always up for doing something new – even blindfold bungee jumping!

* Love a booty call (only she's the one calling for hot, passionate sex).

* Are comfortable in their own skin and cannot be made to feel bad.

* Never make decisions based on fear, especially fear of losing a man.

* Have lots of friends – they know the benefit of the Sisters Support Network!

* Enjoy a good flirt with a handsome young stranger.

Scaredy Cats ...

* Bend over backwards for their boys.

* Wait for their cub to phone and get hysterical if he's late.

* Never go to parties on their own.

* Become shy with attractive members of the opposite sex.

* Never stick to their own point of view.

* Are easily deceived by an over-charming cub.

* Cringe whenever oral sex is suggested.

The Kindest Cut

Often the celebrity cougar will resort to extreme measures to maintain her confidence. Demi Moore, Susan Sarandon, Courtney Cox, Cher, et al., are all streamlined, smoothed-out and reconfigured versions of their former selves, which keeps them looking and (feeling) young. And all of these women have gone the cosmetic surgery route. When it comes to improving on Mother Nature, being a human pin cushion (whether Botox, collagen or any injecting procedure) or even going under the knife, a confident cougar always makes this decision for herself.

- Never listen to anyone who says you don't need it/will look like a human wind tunnel. If you want it, go ahead.

- But whatever you decide to have done, always research, research, research, first!

- Find a reputable surgeon, one with appropriate affiliations. Talk to women who have had the same surgery, surf the Internet – it's your face, after all.

- Be clear about what you want. Some unscrupulous surgeons may try to sell you more procedures than you need so you end up with the face and body of a 17-year-old … and a second mortgage.

- Make sure you follow any aftercare advice – such as sleeping with your head propped up on a pillow.

- A clever cougar never spills the beans. Tell everyone that you're going on vacation for a while and stay tucked up indoors until the swelling has gone down and you feel ready and rejuvenated to go outside.

- When people tell you how remarkably healthy and young you look just smile and say "Amazing health spas these days!"

So, How Cougar-tastic Are You?

Read through the following statements to see which one best describes how you feel. Follow your instincts, then ring either A or B. Find out how you score by totalling the number of As and Bs.

1 I have never been accused of throwing myself at someone.
Agree **A**   Disagree **B**

2 I'm constantly looking for signs that my partner loves me.
Agree **B**   Disagree **A**

3 I always think people can see my faults.
Agree **B**   Disagree **A**

4 I'm often embarrassed about things I have done.
Agree **B**   Disagree **A**

5 I consider myself a lot of fun to be around.
Agree **A**   Disagree **B**

6 People always seek out my company.
Agree **A**   Disagree **B**

7 If I could change the past, I would.
Agree **B**   Disagree **A**

8 I love getting ready for parties!
Agree **A**   Disagree **B**

9 I tend to avoid new social situations.
Agree **B**   Disagree **A**

10 When things go wrong, it's often my own fault.
Agree **B**   Disagree **A**

11 Criticism from others upsets me.
Agree **B**   Disagree **A**

12 I never complain about bad service in restaurants.
Agree **B**   Disagree **A**

13 I'm always busy doing new things.
Agree **A**   Disagree **B**

14 I love to flirt with new people.
Agree **A**   Disagree **B**

15 I smile a lot.
Agree **A**   Disagree **B**

16 I feel guilty when I say no, or say no and then
second-guess myself.
Agree **B**   Disagree **A**

17 After an argument, I'm always the first one to apologize.
Agree **B**   Disagree **A**

18 I always want lots of reassurance and attention from people.
Agree **B**   Disagree **A**

19 Often I wish I could be more like other people.
Agree **B**   Disagree **A**

20 I always think other women have a better figure than me,
even when they don't.
Agree **B**   Disagree **A**

16 or more Bs

Often you're plagued by feelings of low confidence and inferiority. Don't try too hard all the time – you're just as important as anyone else! Fear of stepping outside your comfort zone and possibly making a fool of yourself in social situations is stopping you from taking up new opportunities to grow and meet new people. So seize the day – after all, what have you got to lose?

Between 10 and 15 Bs

While not overwhelmed with feelings of low confidence, you're all too ready to blame yourself when things go wrong. Don't be so hard on yourself: you're probably much more fun to be around than you assume. Learn to project yourself and say what you think/feel instead of always holding back. You'll be surprised how good it feels!

Between 5 and 9 Bs

You are in conflict: while confident in some situations, there are some things that are holding you back. So face the fear: you're still overly influenced by what others think and a bit too ready to cave in when things go wrong. It's only when we can accept rejection and/or criticism without any loss to our self-esteem that we are truly cougar-tastic.

Between 0 and 4 Bs

Hey, not much fazes you! Confident in social situations, you're also unlikely to back down from a fight. You see yourself firmly in the centre of the frame and no one gets the better of you. But be careful: others blessed with less confidence might start to resent you for being the life and soul of the party.

3
Cougar-licious!
The Irresistible Cougar

"I'm very definitely a woman and I enjoy it."

Marilyn Monroe

A true cougar totally embraces her sexuality and youthful
spirit in defiance of grey hair and gravity. After all, women
in their 40s these days are as healthy and attractive as their
mothers were at 30 – and a cougar's not afraid to show it
off. Always prepared, groomed and beautifully dressed, even
if she has just staggered bleary-eyed from the Ritz Carlton
with bed-head hair, she's always got her act together. She's
a cougar, and she knows that by making the best of herself,
she'll stay ahead of the pack.

Get into Tip-top Hunting Condition

Here's your seven-point preparation plan. Follow this step-by-step guide and acquire some healthy habits to help you feel and look in prime fighting form.

Figures matter. First, take a cue from the famous women who have all stepped out with younger men: Demi Moore, Maria Carey, Eva Longoria, Cher ... They all have younger men in common and they all take care of their bodies.

Ditch the bad habits. Break those bad behaviours that are holding you back from being the cougar-licious woman you want to be! Before you reach for that third glass of Sauvignon/choccy bar or cupcake, think how great you would look in that halterneck dress/top you recently spotted. Do you really need it?

Avoid the telly trap. Just walking away from the box keeps you fit and happy. Too much TV not only numbs the brain, it can also cause depression. Studies by scientists in Norway also say that watching too much TV is bad for the heart. What's more, it uses practically zero calories and all those foodie ads encourage you to snack. Switch it off now!

Get bodytastic! OK, so you don't have the body of a woman half your age or pound the parks 24/7, but cougars are still lithe, sexy women who look as if they care about their bodies. Take the stairs more often, park farther away from the store's entrance to work out those legs, go to the gym regularly or take yoga/pilates sessions, jogging, or whatever you enjoy. Sneak in a little extra exercise to work that body of yours.

Mind matters. The brain is one of the body's sexiest organs and learning new things keeps you young at heart. Mental fitness improves alertness, just as jogging enhances the body. So, read the newspaper, listen to the news, complete a crossword or two or learn new vocabulary.

Get rid of the grey! Going grey may be liberating, but it's also ageing and young men are scared stiff of it! Reach for the bottle or go to a professional. Either way, highlights will knock at least 10 years off you and soften the face to boot. And if you do spot a rogue grey hair sprouting out "down there", don't panic as Samantha did in *Sex and the City*: chances are he'll be so swept away by your sex appeal, he won't even notice!

Food for thought. Eat as many nutritious superfoods as you can – think pulses, greens, fruit and fibre. Not only do they make your skin glow, your eyes sparkle and your hair shine, they'll also provide you vital energy and help keep you slim. Try this little the mantra: "Six glasses of water a day will keep the doctor away".

Regular grooming. Keep your skin shiny and young-looking with regular exfoliation and moisturization. Like a facelift, having your brows regularly shaped and waxed takes years off you. Give yourself a home facial once a week (you can make your own with olive oil, lemon and salt). Looking like you care shows that you take pride in yourself.

"I loathe narcissism but I approve of vanity."

Diana Vreeland

Anti-ageing Tips

(and nothing to do with creams!)

Walk with va-va voom. Walking with swinging hips and general "attitude" is seen to be sexy. Flexibility is what makes people appear to "walk young" and you'll find that having a spring in your step makes you feel lighter.

Get out the giggle pin. There is nothing sexier than a woman laughing out loud. It lights up her face with a childlike joy and acts like a neon sign flashing, "I'm a woman who is fun to be around".

Gossip galore. Shush! Have you heard that having a good old chin-wag with friends or family can make you look and feel younger? According to scientists at Knox College in Galesburg, Illinois, a woman is happier and healthier if she enjoys a regular chat with a female friend because this reduces levels of anxiety and stress.

Spend time around young children. Their innocence, spontaneity and infectious spirit is as good as a pot of anti-ageing cream.

"My body's falling so fast, my gynaecologist has to wear a hard hat."

Joan Rivers

Passion Rules

There is nothing that makes you feel and look more youthful than feeling good about life. We all have to deal with the daily hassles but sometimes it does us good to step back from the everyday grind and get in touch with our inner desires. How you get a youthful glow is by finding out what makes you tick. So, do you live life with a passion? Say yes, if you …

* Dance around the kitchen naked.

* Don't take yourself too seriously.

* Walk barefoot on the grass.

* Always have a bottle of champagne or sparkling wine chilling in the fridge – you are party-ready!

* Book a weekend to Rome on the spur of the moment.

Say no, if you …

* Get neurotic if you're not in bed by 10 pm.

* Wear earplugs to nightclubs or concerts if the music gets too loud.

* Refuse to smile because it gives you wrinkles.

* Still want the honed body of a 25-year-old. It's impossible after 40, so get over it!

Five Things Every Passionate Cougar Should Know

1 Ditch the grim "I've-had-a-hard-day expression" – it will age you 10 years. No one likes a woman who has turned cold and cynical. Live in the moment, life is short. Who cares?

2 Be spontaneous: The unknown, unplanned and on-the-spur-of-the-moment are exciting in that you cannot control every detail of what will happen and you simply have to go along with it. Set aside planned activities to allow time to explore and be free. Lie in a field/comfy bed (depending on the season) and daydream. Let thoughts flow freely through your mind and set the happy hormones free.

3 There's something decidedly sexy about a woman who believes. Actress Susan Sarandon has served time in jail in the name of public outrage and men love her all the more for it. The passionate woman sends an arrow to a man's heart.

4 Open the door to your darker fantasies. You don't need vials of blood à la Angelina Jolie (she famously carried ex-husband Billy Bob Thornton's blood around her neck), but awakening your primal self will make you feel alive. And every younger man loves to get to know a bad girl.

5 Be scentaliscious. There's nothing that makes you feel more passionate than wearing a fragrance you love. Whether it's the smell of newly mown grass or fresh flowers, there's a perfume out there that will awaken your inner spirit.

An Irresistible Cougar is Always Prepared

Hey, it's a jungle out there. You never know when a gorgeous toy boy is just around the corner/in the supermarket/at the gym/standing by the bus stop. That doesn't mean you have to go prowling round with your tongue hanging out – it's just better to look good at all times. A canny cougar never leaves the house …

Wearing her pyjamas. Even if she's just popping out for the newspaper.

With stains on her clothes. It will make him think she's a spinster with a house full of smelly pets.

Laddered tights (pantyhose). *So* slatternly!

Greasy hair, cracked lips, dirty fingernails or scuffed heels. If she doesn't care, why should he?

Baggy clothes. Even if she's going to the gym – the only place to look scruffy is indoors while having private female down-time.

Hairy legs/armpits. She may think that spending her money on legs that never get stroked is a bit of a waste. Nevertheless, a savvy cougar is always prepared.

With no make-up. Just a brush of mascara and a dab of crimson lippy can give a tired face that extra zing that will make a hot young himbo come hot on your heels.

Laden down. Try not to weigh yourself down with lots of shopping bags (maybe just one from Gucci) or you could end up being a bit bag lady – it's not very eco-friendly either.

Cougar Emergency Kit

It might be good to get together an emergency kit to keep you prepared and glamorous at all times.

- Bronzing powder to give yourself a healthy glow. Even if you've just had two hours' sleep, or have a hangover.

- A clean pair of panties for the next morning. Some cubs are just too hard to resist!

- Mouth freshener/mini toothpaste and toothbrush kit. After all, coffee breath is never alluring.

- Lipgloss to give you that instant kiss-alicious appeal.

- Pocket book on philosophy. You might need a prop and young men love to be impressed by a woman's brain.

- Baby wipes. If you get all hot and sweaty, rivulets of mascara running down your cheeks will not endear you to him.

- Condoms, lubricant and a card for a cab company in case you want to make a speedy exit.

"It's better to be dead than unkissable." *Helen Rowland*

Unleash Your Inner Sex Kitten

There you are, standing in front of the mirror. Crimson lippy? Check. Lacy Wonderbra? Check. Little Black Dress, heels, lipgloss? Check, check. Preparing to be a toy-boy temptress is all about getting ready for the hunt.

Kitten Girl is the one we all feel like after buying a new pair of dangerously high heels, or when we feel playful and self-indulgent. Sometimes she gets buried under layers of shopping, work and other sensible stuff. With just a few tweaks to your daily routine, you'll be finding your inner sex kitten in no time at all.

Think yourself pretty and you will seem even more so. Did you know that 80 per cent of women think they are fat and that includes celebrities, says a *New Woman* survey. To unleash your sex appeal, you need to appreciate yourself inside and out. Look in a full-size mirror and find five things that make you feel good about yourself. Take note of your physical attributes (eyes, lips, hair, legs, smile) and your style (hairdo, clothing, stance, make-up) and then concentrate on your good bits.

Bump and grind. Get in the mood to play! Find some music that makes you feel sexy. This can be anything that puts you in the mood for dancing. Clear a private space to practise some basic moves. Now bump your hips from side to side, shaking your bootie in time with the music and really let yourself go.

Make a diva entrance. Before you walk into a party, stop and take a few deep breaths. Make sure your posture is good and that you have a smile on your face. Look around as if it's your party: this will give you an air of confidence and relaxed control. As you walk, keep your hands by your sides. Don't rush across the room – you want to appear to be gliding along like a cat. Check out the old Hollywood movies: the main actress always makes a statement entrance.

Get the Soft-focus Sex Kitten Look

- 🐾 For instant sex kitten appeal, create a feline eye in black eye pencil, or chocolate brown for those with paler colouring. Elongate the eyelids by drawing one line above the top lashes and another under the lower ones, sweeping upward and into a point at the outer corner of each eye. Now drag out the line along the eyes. As a finishing touch, apply tons of mascara. Miaow!

- 🐾 Everyone needs some colour in the face. Use cheek creams in peach, pink and berry shades to give a healthy glow!

- 🐾 Get out the lippy and make sure it's red. Yes, your lips look like a vagina (and according to some scientists too)! Need I say more?

- 🐾 Finish off with a lipgloss with a pearlized finish. This amplifies your pout and adds instant glamour.

"Lipstick was the most fascinating thing to me because it was red and got the most attention. Also, it went on the mouth, which I figured was about the sexiest part of a woman that was all right to show in public."

Dolly Parton

Get in the Game

Always wear outfits that make you look irresistible. As every sex kitten knows, where there is sex so there will be power. While the cougar may be signalling she's game, there's no doubt who has the upper hand.

- You don't have to wear black over-the-knee boots, crotch-less panties or crack the whip to get a young man hot for you. Lacy bits and bobs, black negligées and even bits of dental floss in crimson are all guaranteed headturners. And even if he doesn't get a peek, there's nothing a cougar likes more than to know she looks great underneath her dress.

- Stilettos put you in touch with your inner vamp, that part of the subconscious that contains our most basic impulses – to eat, sing and perform the Dance of the Seven Veils at 3 am. Stilettos make you wiggle like Marilyn Monroe … and make young men go crazy and want to whisk you away. A pair of five-inch spikes is associated with feminine glamour and true sex appeal. What's not to like?

- Red is the colour of sex and passion. Scientists report that the male heartbeat goes up at the sight of a glamorous red dress. Also, a backless dress that scoops down low enough to show a teensy-weensy bit of bottom will get you all the attention.

- A stare-worthy cleavage has more currency than the Crown Jewels! Young men are obsessed with your two-bosom buddies and will do almost anything to cop an eyeful. Get yourself properly measured and showcase them in a great bra. You can go up or down a cup size without knowing it. By pushing the breasts upward and together in a specially designed garment, the breasts appear rounder, firmer and plumper – like two pillows your cub can rest his head on. Or go for gold and push together with just enough friction to start a forest fire.

- We all have that dress/top that makes men want to rip it off us. It's called our "result" dress, the one that manages to transform us. If you find one, buy it in different colours – it's worth the investment.

Just How Cougar-tastic Are You?

Are you a cute kitty or a bit of an alley cat on the tiles? Read each statement below and tick whether you agree or disagree to see how you score.

1 As the years go by, I spend more time in the gym/exercising.
Agree **A**   Disagree **B**

2 I always try to look attractive around the house.
Agree **A**   Disagree **B**

3 I feel jealous when I see women with a good figure.
Agree **B**   Disagree **A**

4 At a party, I enjoy going up to new people.
Agree **A**   Disagree **B**

5 People stare at me when I walk past.
Agree **A**   Disagree **B**

6 I don't mind lying on a beach with lots of good-looking people.
Agree **A**   Disagree **B**

7 Sure, I think I make a good leader.
Agree **A**   Disagree **B**

8 It's hard to laugh at myself.
Agree **B**   Disagree **A**

9 Self-improvement is very enjoyable.
Agree **A**   Disagree **B**

10 Often I feel self-conscious in new situations.

Agree **B**   Disagree **A**

11 I am always up for getting out my best silky robe and inviting my boy round.

Agree **B**   Disagree **A**

12 I hate having my photo taken.

Agree **B**   Disagree **A**

Ten or more Bs

Right now, you don't consider yourself at all cougar-tastic! This means you avoid meeting new people for fear of rejection. You are scoring highly on poor body image, something that might be holding you back from being your most attractive you. If you don't feel it, fake it – no one will know!

Between 7 and 10 Bs

You consider yourself below average on the cougar-tastic scale and are on the lookout for affirmation. Get some more self-belief by trying a few new exercise classes, go jogging or take up a yoga session. You know you have the potential – you need a bit of a nudge!

Between 4 and 7 Bs

You think you are above average in the attraction stakes and you seem to be someone that others take notice of. You can be a little shy when meeting new people, but you like to be playful.

Between 0 and 4 Bs

Hey, you have an extremely positive view of yourself and your personality. You enjoy life and you don't take yourself too seriously. You're convinced of your own cougar-tastic charm and so you go out of your way to meet new people.

4
All About the Boy

"Hey there, big boy – come up and see me sometime."
Mae West

The older woman/younger man combo can be the perfect relationship, whether you want frantic sex or a post-divorce pick-me-up and sometimes it's even for keeps. Let's start with a look at the biological facts. The male of the species hits his sexual prime in his late teens whereas for a woman, everything kicks off in her late 40s. You don't have to be Einstein to do the math.

So, what's in it for the older woman? Quite a lot, really. OK, a toy boy may not know his way around the wine list but undressed he looks like Michelangelo's *David* and he's fun, fit and wrinkle-free. Now you need to understand him a bit better.

Things You Should Know About Younger Men

- In plentiful supply and always willing, they're the best thing to shore up a post-divorce ego.

- What they lack in *savoir faire*, they make up for with enthusiasm and optimism. What's more, they will laugh at all your jokes and look at you doe-eyed.

- They have cute, firm butts and their equipment *always* works (more than once a night, even the morning after, should you so desire. And they are happy for you to pass on the benefits of your experience without it damaging their ego (unlike old codger below).

- Full of hope, their hearts are eager and unscarred … but they don't have a penny to rub together!

- If you go on holiday, be prepared for all your snaps to end up on Facebook!

- Don't be surprised if he's glued to his BlackBerry/iPad when you are lounging on the beach and be prepared for lots of twittering and texting.

- He'll still have his own hair and he hasn't turned grey … but he wears way too much hair gel. He could still be sporting braces too.

- And he won't have a middle-aged gut or hairs sprouting forth from his nostrils and ears.

- He'll never want to leave the party early and he loves hearing you talk about the D.I.S.C.O. days. You may both like Sister Sledge, but the big difference is that he doesn't know you're hearing it second-time around and it's not even the original artist.

- You're not his mum, so don't take in his laundry even if he asks nicely.

- His idea of haute cuisine is a two-for-one at a pizza/burger chain and a bottle of Becks.

- He may wear his trousers round his knees. *He* thinks it's cool, so leave him be!

Things You Should Know About Old Codgers

"It's not the men in my life, it's the life in my men." *Mae West*

With a mid-life crisis in full swing and possibly an accompanying dose of erectile dysfunction too, could it be that the appeal of old codgers (and by that, I mean men from 40-ish to 60-ish) is on the wane? Besides, a lot of cougars are just too hot for men their own age to handle. Anyway, if history is anything to go by then it would seem the codger may prefer a willing younger women, someone more easily impressed, who won't threaten their already-fragile waning ego. Here's what you need to know about the older man.

- It's highly likely they're stuck in a mid-life crisis. After all, their testosterone has been diminishing for at least 10 years.

- Some of them will be threatened by your success/intellect/outgoing personality. In short, anything that challenges and perhaps poses a threat to their already-fragile egos.

- Often they wear leather jackets, cowboy boots and Levis and ride Harley-Davidsons. They will say things like "Traffic, Daddy O!" In short, they'll do anything to reclaim their youth.

* Almost certainly, they will have at least one (or even two) ex wives and a gang of children in the background and who's to say they don't still have a wife in tow.

* Unless he's Harrison Ford, he'll have a receding hairline, a stomach like a medicine ball and bushy eyebrows too!

* He'll take you to nice restaurants, but you have to order off-menu because of his ulcer and have Perrier water because he can't drink.

* Somehow the TV remote is surgically connected to his hand and he's bound to shout angrily at the screen (as he argues with the news readers).

* You'll find hair dye on the bed; he's also prone to a mid-afternoon slump (which means he often has to take a nap, which in turn leads to snoring sessions).

* If you can overlook the hip replacement and dodgy knees, he'll probably be set in his ways. After all, you can't teach an old codger new tricks!

* He may expect you to oil the wheels of his corporate life, entertaining his boss and colleagues to elaborate sit-down dinners.

* And he might have a penchant for antiqueing/old boats or tinkering with classic cars, which means you could find yourself scouring musty old antique shops or, worse still, spending Sundays in a freezing-cold boatyard when you could be having brunch in a trendy urban café.

* You could find yourself in the role of unpaid secretary, reminding him of his ex-wife's/childrens'/parents' birthdays and any other out-of-work appointments.

* If you've landed a DILF (Dad I'd Like To F**k) he's bound to feel the loss of his dwindling sexual power. So much so that if any woman under 45 hits on him he'll let you know about it … and then hit the gym like a whirling tornado in a desperate attempt to get those muscles back where they belong!

If all that sounds too much like hard work, try a younger model, but first check out these general guidelines. When it comes to younger men …

* Avoid saying, "When I was young, like you" – or he'll think you're his mother.

* Never stay over at his place: just think of those dirty sheets and the fact that you'll have to queue with at least five of his house-mates to use the bathroom in the morning.

* Don't talk about your work when you're with him. Chances are, he doesn't have a job. Even if he does, he certainly won't understand yours. There are always exceptions, so never chat up your boss's son – unless it's your leaving party or he's so good-looking that he's worth losing your job for!

* Never say things like, "Hey, Duuude!" (or put little smiley faces on your texts). He likes you precisely because you're older.

* Avoid the father-and-son dating combo. Yes, I know men do it all the time, but have some dignity!

* Just don't ask when you'll see him again. He's young, he won't be thinking about the future. Enjoy the moment!

Know "Young Guy Talk" (or YGT)

Younger men don't always have the confidence to say what they mean, and sometimes they're just plain confusing. Make sure you understand their lingo before you go out on the hunt.

What he says ...	**What he means ...**
What do you do for a living?	How much do you earn?
Let's make a plan	For today or tomorrow, not the rest of our lives
You look fit	You look gorgeous
Wanna massage?	I'm feeling horny
I'm going on the computer	You're talking too much
I'm gonna blaze	I'm about to smoke a joint
I've just lost my job	Fancy being my sugar mama?
My mother has one just like that	You're too old. I'm outta here!

"I'm not just a boy toy – I have feelings and dreams like everybody else."

Jon Stewart

Seven Reasons to Date a Younger Man

(Apart from the Great Sex!)

Still unsure? Below are just seven of the many reasons why you should try a younger guy.

1 He's always willing to please. Many younger men appreciate having gained an older woman's interest and trust, which means they can be extremely eager to please. He might even rush out for luxury chocolate ice cream at 4 am, pick you garden flowers and will be attentive if you come down with the sniffles.

2 He is never boring. When you date a younger guy, there's always so much to chat about! As he's still sweet and hopeful, he's bound to be more open and interested in all the things you have to tell him. Why sit opposite a jaded old codger, going on about his receding hairline and expanding mortgage, when you can discuss the latest sounds with a delicious toy boy?

3 He is cost-effective. Instead of dining à la Carte with stuffy waiters and overpriced gourmet, your younger guy will take you to the new burger place or for a picnic in the park and show you how much fun the simple life can be.

4 He is free-spirited. Young and free, his energy is contagious, especially if you've been around men your own age. The younger man is more into life experiences such as walking barefoot on the beach and talking till dawn.

5 **He has more energy than a Duracell.** What lover boy lacks in expertise, he makes up for in enthusiasm and energy. While your friends have to schedule date nights, the toy boy is ever ready, at his sexual peak and always eager to learn new tricks.

6 **He's malleable.** So you're a cougar and, like a lot of confident women, you know what you want and you like to have your own way. A younger man is more likely to go with the flow. Unlike some older men who might bark orders at you, he'll love it when you take the lead and choose the film/vacation/restaurant. Besides, more often than not, it's you who will be picking up the tab.

7 **He is more affectionate.** Those cougars licking their wounds after a painful break-up will find a younger man a sweeter alternative to overdosing on chocolate and Rom-Coms. If he likes you, he'll shower you with affection, little gifts – even a tender massage. Unlike you, he's not yet jaded by broken romances but full of hope and sparkle – he'll compliment you till you feel like a princess. He'll be nice to your friends too.

"Young men want to be faithful, and are not;

old men want to be faithless, and cannot." *Oscar Wilde*

Cubiquette

Young, fit and just waiting for you to pounce … So who are these young men parading around? Follow our guide to finding the cub that most suits you.

Alpha Cub

Good-looking and charismatic, Alpha Cub (AC) is a boost to any post-divorce/middle-aged ego. He might brag about the size of his bonus/condo, but with his privileged background, Gold Amex and enough cocksure swagger to knock lesser cubs out of the way, he is covetable prey. Into status and power, he will try hard to be number one. Avoid if you are feeling low on cougar confidence.

Dating Pros:

AC is the ultimate designer accessory. Well-groomed and dripping with masculine allure, he will double your social stock and cement your place as the Cougar du Jour. He loves playing the hero and will go to any lengths to impress you. His gifts most probably come from Burberry or Prada and he'll always secure a table at the newest, swankiest restaurant in town.

Dating Cons:

With an ego the size of a small country and a wallet to match, this cub is a real player and may well be simultaneously hunting several cats. What with the gym, the NASDAQ and his eagerness to climb the corporate ladder, you may find yourself being fitted into his busy schedule – not something any cougar worth her claws takes kindly to!

Cute Cub

The sensitive cub comes with an entire set of bonding skills and is likely to put your needs before his own. He'll make you feel cherished and understood. This is a great one to go for if you have recently suffered some heartache. Despite the age difference, he's heavily into commitment and you'll be the only cat in the jungle.

Dating Pros: More romantic than a slushy novel, don't be surprised if he serenades you under your balcony, draws you a bath sprinkled in rose petals and falls deeply in love with you after date two. A gentle creature, he has often been used and abused by younger cats and will be so grateful for any show of affection that you'll soon have him eating out of your paw.

Dating Cons: Do you really want a pining, lovesick puppy on your doorstep? If you persist with this one, he'll need lots of emotional support: kind and caring tendencies can easily slip into needy and insecure!

Sporty Cub

This hunk of perfectly toned young meat is the ideal prey if you're into the body beautiful. More likely to spend all his time pumping iron at the gym, he'll look like a demi-god, with the energy of a Duracell battery. Get past his body narcissism – his bathroom shelf is crammed with so many products that he could open a duty-free – and he's dynamite prey. Don't stalk this jock unless you've been working hard with your personal trainer. (He could even be your trainer, like Madonna/ Carlos Leon.)

Dating Pros: Stronger than his rivals, he will be constantly showing off his physical prowess. He'll always carry your shopping, carry you over muddy fields and open that tricky jar (as long as it's not cookies). His combined athletic ability and a competitive spirit ensure he'll be the best sex you've ever had – he's bound to score a hat-trick too!

Dating cons: He might be something of an armchair enthusiast, constantly checking the football/soccer results and watching his carbs/ protein intake. Not only that, but if he has a match/marathon the next day, he'll be off the sex/drink and trot off to bed at 9 pm.

Culture Cub

A musician, artist or even a writer, the Culture Cub (CC) is the perfect hip accessory. His tortured air, flamboyant style and slightly dishevelled demeanour all add up to captivating prey. He'll take you to art-house movies, obscure galleries and explain the finer points of Post-War Existentialism, whether you like it or not, any time of the day or night. Not one to date if you're often tired out after a hard day at the office.

> **Dating Pros:** Most probably he'll have read the Kama Sutra inside out (intellectuals are into pushing the boundaries, even in bed) and will get you into all sorts of uncompromising positions. Brimming with bright ideas and intellectual know-how, he will impress your friends and be the ideal dinner-party guest.

> **Dating Cons:** Don't confuse the passion of an artist with commitment. He's bound to fall madly in love with you – that is, until another cougar inspires his admiration and becomes his muse. He won't have any money and he won't mind if you pick up the tab – always. Intellectuals are high on the finer things in life, low on masculine pride. Indeed, he probably sees it as a fair exchange for his brilliance.

Techi Cub

Obsessed by all things digital, he may have invented 100 operating systems but when it comes to wowing your friends at a glittering gathering, don't hold your breath! With his childlike love of *Star Trek*/Xbox, Techi Cub is a bit of a social newborn and you'll have to show him the ropes. If you can prize him away from his computer, there's bound to be a sensitive soul lurking below those glasses and never-touched-shampoo hair.

> **Dating Pros:** Like all his fellow techies, this nerdy youngster might be about to become the next dot-com millionaire. Besides, if he knows his way around a mouse, then you can teach him how to navigate round you.

> **Dating Cons:** Welded to his gadgets, he could be a dull dining companion. Tell him the restaurant bans anything digital and teach him the art of voice communication. He may be so used to a diet of online porn and computer game heroines that he'll expect you to perform like Lara Croft!

Caddish Cub

He may be young, but don't let that charming smile fool you. CC is a master of seduction. A smooth-talking predator, he is versed in the art of flattery. Always well turned out, he has the elegance of James Bond, the charm of Errol Flynn and the excitement factor of a young Mick Jagger. Be warned. This one is hard to resist. Because, and here's the thing: CC is out to get what he can and he'll treat you (and any other woman) with total disregard for your feelings. If you can play him at his own game, he can be a great way to inject a bit of fun into the day.

Dating Pros: When CC has you in his sights, he behaves as if no one else in the world exists. His attention is like an Exocet missile of love and you are its target. Quite simply, you are the most fascinating creature he has ever set eyes on. Take it for what it is. Caddish Cubs are perfect for great sex with no strings attached. After all, they're never there in the morning to talk about their feelings.

Dating Cons: Often penniless, his desire for instant gratification makes him spend any moolah he has before scheming how he can get more. Be on your guard or, before you know it, he'll wipe out your bank account. Remember, CC is always a womanizer and you are just another notch on his four-poster bedpost.

"Men are luxuries, not necessities."

Cher

Mind the Gap!

The generational gap is something to bear in mind when you're dating a younger man. With some, it may be a minor chasm but others will feel like a gaping abyss. Knowing what you're dealing with can help you avoid any little misunderstandings.

The Early 20s

A fresh feast, full of fun, hope and excitement, he'll jumpstart any flagging confidence or libido. Most probably, he can't believe his luck and will treat you like a goddess.

> **Reality Check:** Expect a rollercoaster of emotions and don't take him at face value: he is still very young, he doesn't know himself yet. Take care not to scare him with your experience – it can be daunting for a boy who is just starting out in life. This age group may not be right for you if you are a cougar licking her wounds.

Mid to Late 20s

He knows his way round the adult world and has probably had his first job/relationship, so he's a little more experienced and sure of himself. Still young enough to be light and fun, he may not have accumulated any baggage yet.

> **Reality Check:** On the flip side, he has a clearer idea of who he is, which means he won't be quite so malleable and not half as much fun. He is beginning to know his own mind and may not roll over quite so easily as the younger cub.

Thirty-something

He's well on the road to knowing who he is and what he wants. If that happens to be you, you'll find him more of an equal. His clubbing nights are probably nearly over, so no need for earplugs 24/7.

> **Reality Check:** He is a man now and his critical senses will be matured. This may be too much like dating a man your own age.

Are You Toy-Boy Ready?

Or perhaps it's time to go back to the classroom ... Complete our fun quiz to find out!

1 Which of the following statements sounds like you:
   a) I have considered dating a younger man.
   b) I have fantasized about taking a younger lover.
   c) I have dated anyone at least eight years younger.

2 How many younger friends do you have?
   a) Most of my friends are the same age or older than me.
   b) I know a lot of young people.
   c) Lots of my friends are younger.

3 How would your friends react to you dating a younger guy?
   a) They'd be surprised, shocked and/or amused.
   b) They wouldn't care.
   c) Most of them are already dating younger men too.

4 Your ideal partner would be ...
   a) Equal to me.
   b) Someone I can have fun with.
   c) Someone who looks to me to make the decisions.

5 What's your attitude to sex?
   a) It's not that important at my age.
   b) It's something I look forward to.
   c) I love it – and want it now!

6 What's your ideal night out?
   a) A dinner party with interesting conversation.
   b) A night out at the cinema.
   c) A rave/concert or anything wild.

7 You ...

    a) Don't have children, but really want them.

    b) Already have kids.

    c) Don't want a family.

Mostly As
Control Bunny

Though intrigued by the idea of dating a younger man, you're not yet ready to take the plunge. You still have issues with letting go.

Mostly Bs
Too Shy, Shy ...

You love the thought of dating a toy boy, but you're still a little too timid to make the first move. Don't worry: take it slow and read on for more techniques.

Mostly Cs
Hot to Trot

Having researched the market, you're good to go! So, what are you waiting for? Go find your toy boy.

5
The Thrill of the Chase

"Dreaming is the poor retreat of the lazy,

hopeless and imperfect lover."

William Congreve

Now you're feeling and looking hot to trot, it's almost time
to get out there to hunt down some fit young prey.
A cougar may be busy or jaded after a long day at the office
but if there's one thing that she loves, it's the
thrill of the chase.

Be a Natural-born Predator

One of the main reasons why some wannabe cougars aren't successful when they go out hunting is simply because they don't become a hunter. Wearing five-inch heels, a dress the size of a hankie and having sprayed your décolleté with more glitter than a disco ball does not a hunter make. To get sharking and flirting fit, first you need to take on a hunting attitude. After all, there's no point in being out-cougared at the initial feeding frenzy!

Top Tips for Boy Baiting

1 **Be determined.** The likelihood of a cute toy boy knocking on your door is slim so don't leave it to chance: get out there! Even if you feel wiped out and all you want is a long, hot bath, we all have those too-tired-to-lift-our-feet-off-the-floor moments. So, put on your favourite music, take a shower and you'll feel hunting fit in no time.

2 **Chick in Charge.** A clever cougar will always try to keep her emotions in check. Even if you are having a few pre-hunt jitters, the trick is to step back for a few moments and get yourself together. Act as though you are an onlooker: in other words, step outside of yourself. When you do this, you step back from how you feel and this allows you to take stock and reboot.

3 **The C word.** Stay committed. Even if you have a busy lifestyle, clear space in your diary for the hunt once a week. Block off the time in red and make a point of sticking to it, even if it does mean letting down your old friend who wants to go shopping for her other half's birthday. Fit young men are far more fun!

4 Cougar-like cunning. Always have a plan. If you are going to a wedding or party, ring up your host in advance and find out about any young men who might also be there. Ask a few questions: what are they like, what do they do? That way, you can prepare some witty things to say. If possible, leave your car at home and then you can ask that nice young man for a lift. Think Mrs Robinson in *The Graduate* – she asked Benjamin for a ride and then sat at the bar of her home, crossing and uncrossing her stockinged legs.

5 Know about popular culture. Read celebrity magazines, listen to the news, and keep up with the latest trends and music. Being in the know will get you a lot of toy-boy brownie points and you may even be able to make sense of his conversation with his friends.

Happy Hunting Grounds

The first rule of any predator when she is out stalking young game is to familiarize herself with the lay of the land. There are plenty of places where you'll find young men. Whether it's the gym, the office or a cyber café, maximize your results by considering all kinds of venues. The following great hunting opportunities will get you started.

First nights: This is a glamorous setting, perfect to display yourself as the irresistible cougar. But don't get drunk on the free champagne or scoff too many canapés … *So* unsophisticated! Note: you'll find similar opportunities at private views, only this time there will be lots of sensitive, arty types.

Singles holidays: Whether you're treking in the Andes or taking part in watersports, adventure holidays are an ideal place to meet young men. The camaraderie is usually great in a group activity and acts as a bonding exercise.

International flights: Flying is just *so* sexy and if he's in First Class, so much the better. But don't join the Mile High Club – it's tacky and only looks good in films. Dress to impress and get yourself upgraded.

On the ski slopes: Do pretend to sprain your ankle just as that handsome ski instructor/snowboarder comes hurtling down the slopes. But don't break a leg just to get a date! Hit the après-ski bars for hot toddies and hot himbos in their ski outfits.

Weddings: All that love in the air… there's certainly something sexy about weddings and with luck, the reception will be heaving with hot young boys.

Evening classes: The cerebral activities of debate, discussion and bonding over Shakespeare/Plato could prove a hot bed for drama and passionate scenes.

At the cyber café: Basically Planet Younger Man, albeit hackers, geeks and students. If you like them studious and introverted, this could be your place. Ditto campuses, only younger, sweeter and *so* sincere! Take your laptop and ask a hot young stud for help.

The weekly shop: Just head for the deli counter or easy-cook healthy meals but be sure he's shopping for one. Steer clear if that basket holds kids' food or female toiletries. You could also take a weekly trip to the launderette and run into a toy boy washing his smalls.

In the rain: If it works, this one has all the hallmarks of romance so offer to share your umbrella or a cab. A real downpour is the perfect excuse to invite him for a hot chocolate in a nearby café. Sit by a window to get the full effect of the rain pounding away on the window panes.

The financial district: Packed full of eligible Gordon Geckos trading shares and looking for lots of fun in the after-hours. You can smell the testosterone overdrive. Go, cougar!

Bookstores, lectures and libraries: Attract his attention with a quote from Aristotle/Plato/Socrates or any other great philosopher/thinker. Either he'll fall in love with you there and then, or think you're completely crazy. Book signings and other literary events are also worth sourcing for prey.

The gym: Full of sweaty male bodies and still more testosterone! Ask a fit young boy to show you how to set the treadmill or to advise you on weights – the opportunities are endless.

At the office: Tricky, but what about the mail/copier boy, or if you like them *really* young, the new intern? Perch on their desk, lean over and watch them blush! Up the excitement factor by keeping the whole thing a secret; most bosses are not keen on office romances. Unless of course, you happen to be the boss!

The Five Stages of Hunting

"Yeah, I flirt! I'm not blind, and I'm not dead."

Dolly Parton

1 The Tender Trap

A cougar knows exactly what she wants (fit young men) and once a suitable prospect is in sight, she does her best to secure it. Here are some tips to help you snare your own tasty prey.

Choose the right victim. When you first arrive at a bar/party/opening, scan the room to take a good look at what's on offer. After all, if you do go after a 25-year-old, stunning male model surrounded by slavering kitties (aka younger females), unless you are very rich or happen to be Madonna, you may find yourself going home with nothing but your tail between your legs. Look for the quiet one in the corner, chomping away on crudités, or the cute, smiley boy chatting with all his mates.

The rule of one. What better way to highlight your looks, charms and talents than hanging out with women who are less attractive and/or charming? No, that doesn't mean you have to choose a wrinkly old Vera to go sharking with, just be sure that when you're at a bar, party or any other event that you stand tall and stand out from your mates.

Good enough to eat. Buy perfume that smells of chocolate, apples, vanilla, cinnamon or mown grass. These are comfort smells and will bring back happy, childhood memories for your cub. They're also a great way to soften him up and make him feel relaxed and open.

Smile. Dating is a numbers game. Smile sweetly at everyone and improve your odds of finding a cub.

2 Cougars Make the First Move ... Fast!

You don't have to rush over to the first fit boy who catches your eye, sit on his knee and plant a wet one. But once you've found your prey, how do you get his attention before some prepubescent kitty wearing a crochet hankie and vertiginous heels slinks into view? A clever cougar is cool. She positions herself close enough to get a good look, then casually wanders over. It's good to have a fellow cougar with you at this time (chatting and smiling is a good look) and with luck, he'll notice you. Just be sure to agree who's going in for the kill!

"From looking, men get to loving."

Clement of Alexandria

3 In for the Kill

You're looking seductive and you're sashaying over to your toy boy. Now's the time to get the chemistry going. As you approach him:

Bedroom eyes: Throw him the "bedroom look". It's longer than a normal gaze and so intense and welcoming that he'll be mesmerized. Then slowly drag your eyes away. Just don't overdo it at this stage: you are telling him you like what you see, not saying come back to mine or anything else! If he looks back at you, raises his eyebrows or gives you a mega-watt smile, he's giving you the green light.

A body for sin: When flirting with potential prey, let your body do the talking. According to scientists 75 per cent of our communication is non-verbal so you can find out what your cub is thinking by following his body language. Study the male sex signals below:

- If you like someone then you tend to move toward them so it's a good sign if his body is pointing toward yours.

- Puffing out his chest means he's trying to look more powerful for you.

- Smoothing down his hair, straightening his tie or pulling his beanie down means he's preening himself to appear more groomed for you.

- Winking shows friendliness and is also a sign that he's quite a cocky cub.

- If he's standing with his legs apart and holding onto his belt, he's not going in for the Cowboy of the Year, he just wants to appear macho.

Looks positive. Now get him thinking about you in the right way with your own sexy signals! Here are a few ideas:

- Head tilt and smile combo: this says, "I've noticed you and I like what I see!".

- Twirling strands of your hair seductively is a real turn-on.

- Remember to stand with your back arched, breasts out.

- Nibbling on your lower lip can be a bit of a tease, but don't bite so hard you draw blood and frighten him away.

- Lick your lips while giving him bedroom eyes. But don't stare too much or you'll look scary.

- Look straight at him then flip your hair.

You may be the most cougar-licious woman in the room, as clever as Hilary Clinton with the wit of Dorothy Parker, but sometimes he just isn't that into you. Here's how to tell if he's not interested:

- He stays talking with his mates. A man will move closer to you, if he is interested.

- He's out of synch with your body language. When someone is into you, he will mimic what you do.

- He talks to you like someone in the office. If he's talking brusquely and quickly, he is talking friend, not lover language!

- On meeting you, he quickly mentions his girlfriend.

Of course there will be other occasions when he thinks you are the most interesting woman on the planet and you wish you were talking to the hot young himbo on the opposite side of the room. There are ways of letting someone down lightly without hurting their feelings. These are effective and fast brush-offs.

* Ask him where he got his hat/shirt because you want to get your son one just like it.

* "Oh, that's my friend Janey," you say, gazing into the middle distance. "Must dash." And with that, you trot off to talk to the ice sculpture.

* Tell him it's been great chatting but you're off to get another drink/circulate.

* If all else fails, just lie: tell him you're seeing someone.

* Or worse, tell him you want to have his babies now!

4 Poised to Pounce

Now that you've read his signals and got him all sexed up, if he hasn't rushed off to the bathroom to check his hair gel or decided to check the texts on his mobile phone, more than likely he wants to get personal.

Always remember, it's not just how you move or the way that you look that might attract the cub of your dreams. Sure, war paint and clingy dresses can increase the odds, but what you say may also get you to the next level. Flattering your prey will soften him up and make him feel good. Keep in mind that compliments should be delicate and lightly given to ensure their staying power. OK, it's time to start talking. Here are my Top 10 Pre-Pounce Openers.

* "See my friend standing over there? She wants to know if you think I'm cute."

* "I just thought you should know that you have a really nice smile/eyes/shoulders."

* "If I could rearrange alphabets, I would put U and I together."

- 🐾 "Is it hot in here or is it just you?"

- 🐾 "Excuse me, is this seat taken?"

- 🐾 "You look like you might be interested in some good conversation."

- 🐾 "That's a lovely tie/shirt/jacket you're wearing (touching said item at the same time)."

- 🐾 "Excuse me, can you help me with this?" Bag/drink, etc.

- 🐾 "Can I interest you in glass of …" (naturally you need a bottle of wine for this one).

- 🐾 "Where's the exit? Will you go out with me?"

- 🐾 "Are those your eyeballs I found them in my cleavage?"

"Flirting is the gentle art of making a man feel pleased with himself."

Helen Rowland

5 Soften Him Up for the Kill

Now you've broken the ice and you and your cute cub are standing at the bar/party/gallery opening chatting away like two turtledoves, use your cat-like skills to make him feel at ease. You may find your young prey is nervous – after all, he won't have the benefit of your experience. So bring him out of his shell and let him tell you all about himself. Pepper your conversation with supportive statements such as "Uh huh, yes I see …" and "how interesting!". It will put him at ease and make him feel special. Here are some more ideas to keep things flowing.

Tickle his fancy. Make him laugh: men love a funny woman. But that doesn't mean you have to wear jokey T-shirts or have stick-on nipples – that's just plain irritating! No, the key to being funny is to be light and amusing. Be playful – no hysterical laughter or screeching or you'll probably end up red in the face. Highlight the funny/dramatic bits of your stories and sprinkle your conversation with witty observations about the people around you (not too bitchy, mind!).

Don't try too hard. Batting your eyelids, telling jokes too loudly and swinging your Gucci handbag around are all a bit like wearing a big neon sign that says: "Desperate and up for it, now!" More than a whiff of desperation and he'll be off. He has to believe you have other things to do, but you chose to talk with him.

Touch a little longer. So it's all going swimmingly and what happens next might possibly nail your prey for the rest of the evening. Perhaps even for life. Accidentally on purpose let a part of your body touch his. It might be your leg that rests against his, or you could reach out and touch his arm/hand when he says something funny/ interesting. Flirt with a soft, seductive voice and watch as your little cub turns to putty.

Sexual No-nos

* Avoid chewing gum: you will look inelegant and seem more like his younger sister/cousin.
* Don't wait for him to buy you a drink. He's young and probably penniless too.
* Laugh like a hyena and you'll look mad/desperate and he'll soon run away.
* Remember, you're too sophisticated to get away with cursing like a drunken lout.
* Don't overeat at the buffet or worse still, stuff sausage rolls in your handbag.
* Always carry breath-freshener in your bag to avoid ashtray/fish/ coffee breath.
* Unless it's gravity defying and properly upholstered, don't have too much cleavage on display.
* Ditto micro miniskirts that are so short you have to keep yanking them down over your thighs.

"It's better to be looked over, than overlooked."

Mae West

Does He Like Me?

When a younger man finds himself consumed with lust for an older woman, he won't always make it obvious. For a start he's probably a little nervous: though you might see yourself as a seasoned old wrinkly, in his eyes you're an unattainable goddess and so he may be scared to make the first move. However, there are some telltale signs that show he likes you.

- He blushes when you look at him. Most probably his sympathetic nervous system is going into overdrive.

- He stands or sits in the open position: that is, facing you with his arms uncrossed.

- Has he moved closer to you and/or touched you subtly, such as patting your hand or a light touch of your cheek?

- Maybe he's flipping beer mats and trying to catch peanuts in his mouth. This means he likes you, but he's really nervous!

- He keeps sneaking glances at you from underneath his hoodie/baseball cap. When someone is really interested, they can't help looking at you.

What's Your Seduction Style?

Before we move onto the next step (and the next chapter), it's time to check out your flirting persona. Couqettish or charismatic, discover what kind of cougar you are with our fun quiz.

1 You fancy your best friend's nephew. Do you …
   a) Put on your result dress and heels and flirt like crazy. It's naughty and that's why it's fun!
   b) Engage in witty banter and get drunk together.
   c) You're playful without realizing it – really, you don't think it's right.
   d) You give him the come-on, but then pull back.

2 What's your chat-up style?
   a) Confident – you zero in on what you want and get it.
   b) Engaging – you draw others in with your wit and personality.
   c) Fun, fun, fun – you get out your playful inner child.
   d) Coy – even though you're a cougar, you like to play hard to get.

3 How would your friends describe you?
   a) Goal-orientated and a wee bit insensitive.
   b) Extrovert, warm but sometimes annoying.
   c) Playful, but shy and slightly needy.
   d) You avoid confrontation and can be a bit passive-aggressive at times.

4 Your best skill is …

   a) You always seem special – in fact, rather grand.

   b) Making others feel sexy and attractive.

   c) Creating a fun atmosphere and enjoying every minute of life.

   d) Tapping into other's emotional needs.

5 Your favourite film is …

   a) *Double Indemnity.*

   b) *Annie Hall.*

   c) *Runaway Bride.*

   d) *Gigi.*

6 While sitting alone at a bar, you spot a handsome cub. Do you …?

   a) Send him over a drink, then give him a sultry smile.

   b) Go to the bathroom and as you pass by, throw him a witty one-liner.

   c) Give him a warm smile and ask if you can join him.

   d) Smile at him, but then ignore him and chat on your phone.

7 What would you wear on a first date?

   a) A tight black figure-hugging dress and high stilettos.

   b) You express how you feel in a flirty dress.

   c) Jeans and a skimpy top.

   d) A beautiful dress that is not over-the-top sexy but shows off all your good bits.

Mostly As
The Siren

Supremely confident, with a highly sexual presence and always dressed to kill, you are the ultimate young male's fantasy. Charismatic and aloof, you appear totally in control. Watch out: you could come across as a bit cold and calculating.

Mostly Bs
Charismatic Seducer

Extrovert and outrageous, you draw in your prey through the strength of your personality. You give off an air of feverish excitement. However that chutzpah might possibly overwhelm him. Underneath it all, you've got a heart of gold and cubs always adore you.

Mostly Cs
Natural Temptress

Playful and childlike, you have a natural spontaneity. You like to act like a child and though you may be older, you make him feel as if he's your big brother. This is a great style for the Cougar Lite who prefers her cub to do the initial pursuing.

Mostly Ds
Coquettish Seductress

You have the ability to hold your victim in your thrall with a hint of what's to come. If you sense he's losing interest, you can quickly disengage but you really focus when his desire is consummate. Be careful: he could tire of your games.

Getting in the game is often the best part of the dating process: you've spotted each other across a crowded room. You've flirted, flattered, danced and drunk cocktails. Hopefully you've swapped numbers and even managed a polite kiss goodnight. Lust is in the air and anything could happen. So enjoy the moment and savour the adrenalin rush before either of you picks up the phone to arrange the first date.

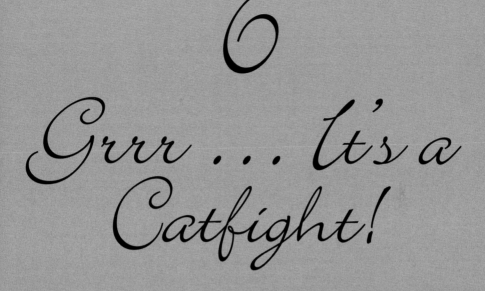

6
Grrr ... It's a Catfight!

"A bitch loves being born. It's her first experience of making another woman scream and cry."

Pamela Stephenson

It's a real (love) jungle out there: wherever hot young himbos wander about, pumas and kitties (younger women in their 30s and 20s respectively) are bound to be lurking in the undergrowth. Any cougar worth her whiskers knows that if she's to stay ahead of the pack, there may be times when she needs to claw her way to the top of the feeding frenzy. It pays to know the laws of the jungle. Here's our step-by-step guide to winning the catfight.

Cougars Versus Kitties

There may be those who may say, "Uh, huh ... a younger man will never be interested in an older women, just look at all the young kitties around." Well, they are wrong. Cougars are an exciting alternative to the younger woman. Independent and glamorous, a cougar often has more in common with her cub than other people might think. After all, they both like having sex, having fun and feeling free. Besides, there are more positives. A true cougar ...

- Knows herself and nothing phases her – not even a bikini-clad bombshell slinking up to her cub.

- Feels good inside: after all, she's been through the bad break-up or the divorce and got the condo in the Hamptons.

- Cuts to the chase and is upfront about what she wants.

- Doesn't want kids or perhaps she's already had them.

- Has a now-or-never mentality: she lives for the moment and will dance till dawn and have sex in an open-top car.

- Has streamlined her social network and doesn't waste time with fair-weather friends or hangers-on.

- Usually wants what her cub wants: sex.

- Has her own house/car and most probably a hot tub, installed just to entertain her cub.

Besides, she'll never have a hissy fit, whine or moan. She's done all that when she was married/living with a partner and now knows it won't get her anywhere!

Then there are the kitties and pumas. Yes, they may have ping-back skin, tight buns and thick "I-want-to-run-my-hands-through-it" hair but many of them treat a first date like a job interview: "How much do you earn?", "Do you like children?".

Chances are, younger men are tired of the demands and ticking biological clocks of their fellow cats. So, what are the characteristics of a kitty or puma?

- She starves herself and eats lettuce leaves when she's dining out or pushes food round her plate.

- Younger women experience a lot of firsts (first love, first betrayal) but this can cause her to be drama-prone.

- She's constantly texting/emailing/calling her girlfriends to get their approval before she makes plans.

- This girl is so insecure that she's always checking herself in the restaurant/bar/gym mirror.

- If her man so much as glances at another female, she'll have a hissy fit.

- She's high maintenance and frets about her cellulite: "Are my breasts/ butt too big? ..."

- On date three or four she'll profess undying love.

Finally, she'll expect guys to do everything for her – and that includes buying her a Prada handbag!

How to Survive a Kitty Attack

It's fair to say that most kitties see young men as their right and will stop at nothing to steal an older woman's prey. Here are some survival tactics.

- When a kitty comes up, don't clutch his arm nervously and drag him away or you'll look like a bunny boiler. Instead, engage in some witty banter – after all, you are older and better at this game.

- Give her the bitch stare and tell her that she has a stain on her derrière if she won't go away.

- If he rubbernecks a few kitties at a party/dinner, go off and talk to an older man/the restaurant owner. Watch how he comes crawling back to you.

- When she talking about some new band/film that she knows you don't know anything about, it's time to pat his behind, give him a feline smile and buy a round of drinks!

Catty Comments

While cougars are out and about having fun with their cubs, kitties can't always cope. After all, they think you're in their territory and they may feel threatened and insecure. You might attract a few remarks such as these:

- ✳ "He must have a mother complex."

- ✳ "What a lovely dress – my mother has one just like it."

- ✳ "Remind me of your age …"

* "Here, let me give you the number of my hairdresser."

* "He's definitely after your money."

* "What a distinctive voice you have – it sounds just like a foghorn."

* "You look great in that dress ... from the side."

* "I've had a lovely time ... but this wasn't it."

* "Lovely top – your nipples stick out like hard peas!"

Don't Get Mad, Get Even

In the face of a kitty attack, the trick is not to get angry or upset. After all, a red-faced and spluttering, hysterical cougar is: a) not a good look, and b) the reaction that kitty was aiming for. Besides, men don't often notice bitchiness between females. You don't want him to think you're a jealous harridan but any cougar worth her claws won't let a kitty get away with an attack. Here are a few pointers:

* Smile sweetly and ask who her favourite artist/writer/thinker is.

* "Isn't it a school night?" you ask.

* Say: "You're quite a wit – well, I was *half* right!"

* Say: "Nice top! It's amazing what you can do with a pair of curtains." Or even, "I just love your dress! Can you lend me the pattern?"

* And if all else fails, "Come and meet some friends of mine," (to him) and lead him away.

Outmanoeuvre at the Feeding Frenzy

It's not only blonde bombshells that you have to watch when you're competing for hot prey. Practised in the art of the attack, your fellow cougars can have cunning ways to swipe your cub from under your nose. If your nose is twitching, watch out there's a cougar about! She will …

- 🐾 Talk about her chalet in Aspen/flat in Monaco and then drop into the conversation that she needs someone to share it with her for the summer months.

- 🐾 Sprinkle the conversation with celebrity names and cool parties she has been invited to.

- 🐾 Touch him subtly when she thinks you're not looking or you've gone to the bathroom.

- 🐾 Place a hand on his thigh and purr in his ear.

- 🐾 Tell you there's a call for you/someone is looking for you just to get you out of the way.

- 🐾 Sprinkle him with compliments such as "Ooh, what a lovely shirt/tie/thighs!"

Reclaim Your Inner Bitch

"I found my inner bitch and ran with her."

Courtney Love

Watch out, the cats are definitely on the prowl! When you put a number of women together and there's something to compete for, such as young hot cubs, the outcome is more than likely to be a full-on cat-calling, hair-pulling bitch fest rather than a sit-down tea party. Because, and here's the thing when it comes to women: we all have an inner vixen lurking beneath our nice-girl exterior dying to get out and beat the competition! Being catty and scheming is part of the female DNA. For us girls, bitching is a way of life. We scheme to get one up at dinner parties/board meetings/supermarket checkouts and on the beach. So why not unleash your inner shrew? You know you want to, really!

A successful bitch …

* Knows how to keep her hairdresser/personal trainer/cub waiting.

* Is never too eager to please. She doesn't do jumping through hoops.

* Wears skyscraper heels and has her pointy nails poised in the event of attack.

* Distinguishes herself from the common herd.

* Is as sweet as a Georgia peach on the outside … and tough as concrete on the inside.

* Can throw a dirty look, filthy enough to make grown men cry!

* Calls everyone her "best friend, daaaahling!" then stabs them in the back.

* Sizes up her opponent's legs/hips/cleavage in a nanosecond and spends the next 10 minutes pulling her apart.

Be a Successful Bitch

**"I have the same goal I've had ever since I was a girl:
I want to rule the world."** *Madonna*

Being a successful bitch doesn't mean you should go around ruining reputations
(or lacerating anyone with a deft whack of your paw). When the stakes are high,
learning the art of subtle bitchery as self-defence against other Cruella de Vils and
staying ahead of the game is vital. After all, it can be a dangerous world out there.

Rule number one: Always be charming when hurling a bitch attack. A bitch
never sounds rude, angry or spiteful: that just makes you look bitter and twisted.
Besides, it's bound to encourage a rival cougar to launch a counter attack.

Rule number two: Smile and mask your own attack with a soft tone of voice or even
better, as a joke. Getting people to laugh with you will take the sting out of her tail.

Rule number three: Remain cool under pressure. Getting all emotional and
teary-eyed because some kitty has floored you a catty remark will only make
things worse. It's important to stay calm – that way, you can think of a witty
counter-sting. Try this the next time you are under fire: step back, go to the
bathroom to reapply your lipgloss, take a few deep breaths to slow your
breathing down, collect yourself and give yourself time to think.

Rule number four: Master the art of feeling out other women's weaknesses.
Read their body language. They sound on top of things but if they are standing
with a stooped gait or they look crestfallen when they think no one is looking at
them, they are not as confident as they are trying to make out. This should make
you feel strong enough to launch a counter attack, if they have lashed out at you.

Rule number five: To get what you want, you need to give the impression
that you don't care two hoots about what people think. Showing your cracks
and vulnerabilities only gives them the perfect opportunity to get out their inner
Imelda Marcos!

How to Avoid a Bitch Fit

"A true friend stabs you in the front."

Oscar Wilde

A really good bitch never loses control, but sometimes when we're up against it even the best of us can feel like breaking out and having a bitch fit. So what do you do?

- If you feel yourself reddening, don't grunt like a pig and stomp your feet. At best, you will look inelegant and at worst, mad.

- Walk away and gather your thoughts. Visit the bathroom and splash your face lightly with cold water. Think about what you are going to do.

- Make a judgment call. Should you say something? If you decide to go ahead, take her aside and do it in private so you don't end up with egg or her Martini on your face.

- Take the high road. Examine if it's really worth getting into a bitch fest. It may be better to cut your losses and leave/move on to another group.

Top Bitch Attacks

Of course we've all been stung by a bitch attack. Like radon gas, they're hard to detect and seem to come out of nowhere until the damage is done and you're left licking your wounds. You may recognize some (or all) of the following:

1 The Bitch Slap
As subtle as a ton of bricks, this one is a full-on, filthy, up-and-down eyeball with lip curling and eyebrow arching followed by a brief but icy stare. Deadly as cyanide, it can floor a fellow cougar at 50 paces. If you're on the end of this one, fight back with a subtle putdown worthy of Cruella de Vil or walk away – there's more to come!

2 Do I have poo on my dress?
Done properly, this one can make the most confident cougar reach for a tissue. The withering glance comes back at you when you say something that you think is funny/interesting. Combined with a deadpan look, it suggests: "I've checked you out and frankly love, I've seen better dirt on the road!"

3 Sneak Attack
Her words might be laced with honey, but make no mistake: you have been well and truly slapped. It goes like this. There you are sipping a cocktail and chatting to your cub. "I don't mean to be a bitch," she says (right!). Now here comes the insult: "but I think you're a bit old for him." Cute bitch's face softens and shows sisterly concern while her voice is seductive and sweet as treacle. Beware: underneath are daggers dipped in cyanide.

4 Mmm ... sorry, you're *so* boring!
This kitty comes up smiling and asks you about your poor Aunt Edna. Before you have time to say "Oh, she's getting better", she's cut you off mid-sentence and is already talking to someone else.

What to Do If You're on the End of a Bitch Attack

Front it. That doesn't mean you have to be the kind of woman who wears a raccoon's penis as a necklace pendant, but dare to be different. Get a dirty laugh and practise a menacing walk to show you're not someone to be messed with. This will make any bitch think twice.

Never take it personally. Don't lick your wounds in front of a group of braying hyenas – you may look like you're in the midst of a whiney panic attack and that will only make things worse. Stay calm and simply smile.

Pick your battles. Sometimes it's better just to ignore the kitty that has tried to freeze you out of the conversation. Let her make a fool of herself and you'll come out smelling like roses.

Take the sting out of their tail. Next time someone tells you that you look just like their Aunt Daisy or you have hair like a brush but you can't think of a suitably acid retort, the best way to diminish their sting is to agree. "Absolutely," you say, smiling like a Cheshire cat. Then watch her slink away, tail between her legs.

"Life's a bitch, and life's got lots of sisters."

Ross Presser

The Three Main Bitches

So, how do you know what you're up against? Meet the three main bitches you're going to have to deal with.

Alpha Bitch

Takes the bitch to a whole new level. The ultimate female predator, she circles her prey, preparing to strike with a voice that could freeze water. She's shady, untrustworthy and thinks nothing of indulging in an A-list bitch-fest before breakfast. Your average megalomaniac with *Dynasty*-esque Krystle-and-Alexis chutzpah, she can wipe out a rival with a swipe of her paw and knife you in the back without blinking.

> **Where to find her:** She's most likely stalking the corridors of multinational companies and screaming at the top of her voice in boardrooms. This bitch is feared and respected in equal measure.

> **What she wears:** Power suits by Donna Karan and other top-name designers. She is always groomed and coiffed, not a hair out of place.

Cutie Pie

Blonde, softly spoken and with the fragile face of an angel, CP is all apple pie and maple syrup on the outside but with a granite-like core. She delights in causing misery (other people's). Practised in the art of seduction and destruction, Cutie Pie is dangerous. You'll find yourself telling her your innermost secrets, but she'll store and use them against you at a later date. Be warned: this one is a top schemer and fakes her vulnerability!

> **Where to find her:** Model parties are full of former CPs, as are opening nights, where she simultaneously simpers, schemes and sips champagne.

> **What she wears:** Low-cut tops, flat ballerinas and she may even carry a Chihuahua in her jewel-encrusted handbag.

Style Queen

This diva looks so cutting-edge it hurts and she's always critiquing the competition. Stay well clear if you are wearing anything baggy/UGG boots or last year's look: she'll give you the withering once-over and then turn to her friends and laugh. She's practised in the art of vile verbal assault (just think of all those bitchy designers she has to deal with). Like a velour tracksuit, avoid unless you also happen to be a fellow Style Queen.

> **Where to find her:** On Dolce & Gabbana's yacht, or any other gay A-lister she can lig off.

> **What she wears:** Head-to-toe in statement fashion, she drips designer and thinks Manolo Blahnik is God.

So, How Bitchy Are You?

Do you just live for gossip and would you betray a friend's confidence at the merest whiff of a scandal? Or are you just too nice to even think about being nasty? Complete our quiz and find out for yourself.

1 How often do you gossip about other people's appearance/love life?
a) Whenever I can – it's fun.
b) Sometimes, when it comes up.
c) Hardly ever! I hate being bitchy – it leaves me feeling funny.

2 Someone tells you a secret about someone else. Do you ...
a) Get on the phone/email and tell colleagues, friends and acquaintances?
b) Mention it only to your closest friends?
c) Tell no one, not even your mother.

3 Your cub is late for a date. Do you ...
a) Get even?
b) Get going?
c) Get him a drink?

4 A fellow cougar turns up at a party wearing an identical dress. Do you ...
a) Accidentally-on-purpose spill a drink over her?
b) Laugh, but make sure you don't stand too close?
c) Tell her she looks *sooo* much better in it?

5 A friend confides in you about something deeply personal. Do you ...
a) Pretend to be concerned, then store it up and use it against her at a later date?
b) Tell her you're tired and could you chat another time?
c) Spend hours counselling her and skip your gym session?

6 It's hard for you to be friendly with other females,
unless they are exactly like you? ...
a) Always.
b) Sometimes.
c) Never.

7 What are you like in a fight?
a) I never apologize and end up making the other person cry.
b) Though fair-minded, I rarely back down.
c) I'm all for a quiet life so I always give in.

Mostly As
Uber Bitch

Time to tone down the bile, sister. You may be on top at the moment,
but no one really wants a bitch as a friend, so watch out!

Mostly Bs
Not so bitchy

Middling on the bitch-o-meter. You lack emotional attachment
and tend to put yourself first. Learn to trust and you may soften up a little.

Mostly Cs
Too nice by half

They don't come nicer than you! Be careful: if you put others before
yourself too often, they'll see you as a pushover and turn on you.

7
The First Date

"Dating is a social engagement with the threat

of sex at its conclusion."

P.J. O'Rourke

So you've snared your prey and numbers have been
exchanged. Now it's that giddy, scary time before the first
date. While even the savviest cougar might think nothing
of chairing conferences in Peru, meeting heads of state,
running a marathon or simply organizing a dinner party,
preparing for a first date with a younger man can be
surprisingly nerve-wracking. After all, such an occasion is
loaded with expectancy. Will the sparks fly? Or will he (or
you) feel like running for the hills? So, how can you ensure
your first encounter is the best it can be? Follow our
step-by-step guide for first-date success.

The Essential Rules of Phone-tiquette

* After a stressful day at the office don't phone a potential date. You could end up sounding like a grumpy old cow, not a confident cougar!

* Do pick a time when you're feeling up and good about life – it will show in your voice.

* Don't drink and dial. A glass of Pinot to pep you up is fine but if you've had an exhausting day and end up downing the whole bottle, hide the phone!

* Be sure to give yourself time to wind down. A bubble bath will make you feel comfortable and in the mood for talking.

* Don't email or text him to arrange a date. It may be easier and less risky, but by avoiding any voice-on-voice contact, you are only building him up in your mind. It could come across as a bit rude too.

* Do keep the conversation light, humorous and short. Ask him how he is, fix the time and date and say goodbye. Job done!

Look Hot to Trot

It's natural to want to look your cougar best on a first date. After all, he's young and handsome with a six-pack and a cute smile and he's probably been boasting to his friends all week about you. Of course you want to look great. Here's how.

* Wear something that makes you feel absolutely fabulous. If you don't feel you have anything in your wardrobe that brings out your inner goddess/is suitable for the occasion, go shopping. He's worth the investment.

- Dress to impress. understated, sexy, maybe a touch of danger. A tight-fitting red/black dress always works and will send his heart rate soaring. If you opt for figure hugging, don't go too short or skimpy: after the age of 25, too much flesh on display looks desperate – you might be in danger of slipping over into hooker territory! Keep the look classy by teaming it with a smart jacket and stilettos. Add sheer stockings and possibly some discreet jewellery that jazzes up the outfit.

- Don't have a different haircut just before the date. You may think it will give you a lift but if it's a disaster you'll spend the entire time feeling so gloomy. You'll be constantly checking yourself in the mirror/ rearranging your "funny fringe (bangs)" so much that your date might think you're a bit loopy. Anyway, he likes the way you look or he wouldn't be meeting you.

- Allow plenty of time to get ready. Take a long bubble bath and moisturize afterwards for soft, kissable skin. Apply your make-up and fragrance with care: too much hair gel/perfume and you'll end up smelling like a pharmacy! Don't experiment with make-up at this stage, go for something that you know works. And avoid foundation/lipstick overkill – remember, less is more.

Location, Location

If you are doing the choosing, pick somewhere you know your cub will like and is age-appropriate. Just because you enjoy Steak Tartare and funk/jazz, it doesn't mean your date will, too! Below are a few possibilities.

Daytime

* Quick lunch or coffee: An hour or two's lunch or a coffee in a little place you know is a great idea when dating a younger man. The advantage of keeping the first date short and simple is that if you find you have nothing in common, you don't have to make it through a seven-course dinner, staring at the floor while he says, "Wassup?" (or even worse, chats up the 21-year-old waitress). Arrange it for a weekend and that way, if you do click, you can take a romantic stroll in the park afterwards.

* The art gallery: All that culture will give you lots to talk about. You may discover your toy boy has an artistic soul lurking beneath his hoodie. Choose the medium carefully. Exciting photographic exhibitions, Pop Art, Andy Warhol, Gilbert and George, anything with a bit of pizzazz might be suitable for the younger male. He might become bored and run off to find his mates. If you've been invited to a private view or you are a "friend" of a gallery with a swish members room, he might enjoy that as an added extra. Not a good date if your cub is strictly hip-hop or an Austin Powers' fan.

Evening

* Movie and a drink afterwards: With minimal talking involved, at least there's no pressure to communicate. You can hold hands in the dark without him seeing you blush and kiss him in the back row. Not so good for getting to know each other, unless you have factored in the post-flick drink-and-chat. Why not choose a cinema with luxury seats/ a bar to impress him?

* Cocktails at happy hour: This date is cub-perfect – fun and flirty, with little pressure attached. If either of you gets first-date jitters, there's the added advantage of alcohol (not too much, mind!) to give you Dutch courage. If you find yourself clock-watching or fiddling with your BlackBerry, you can always make a quick getaway.

* Dinner date: Tried and tested, dinner at a romantic restaurant can be the elixir of first dates. If he has decided on this one, he obviously thinks you are a trophy cougar and is proud to be seen with you, so be brave! On the other hand, you're both locked into a two-hour rom-marathon and nothing short of a phone call from your best friend/babysitter will get you out of it. It could be an uncomfortable ride if you're none too sure about the boy.

"I've been on so many blind dates, I should get a free dog."

Whitney M. Young, Junior

On the Date

Making an Entrance

Creating a good first impression will show you're a confident cougar and win the affection of your cub. Just follow these tips.

- Taking a cab is probably the best idea when you're going on a date that involves dressing up. Avoid the risk of arriving hot and flustered from the subway and/or looking like a racoon with rivulets of mascara running down your face.

- Don't wear shoes that you can't walk in. You'll feel uncomfortable and look inelegant, especially if you end up walking like Max Wall! You'll be thinking about your sore feet, not your date. Besides, if you end up taller than him, he'll feel more emasculated than big swinging toy boy.

- Don't wear anything too tight. If it splits, you might spill your Cosmopolitan or worse still, end up in the bathroom for the entire date.

- Arrive at least 10 minutes' late: this should ensure your toy boy is already waiting for you at the bar. If he isn't there when you arrive, flirt with the cute waiters and make him sweat!

- Be the one to break the ice. After all, he's younger than you and bound to be a bit nervous. Kiss him "hello" on both cheeks, smile and compliment him.

> "I require only three things in a man: he must be handsome, ruthless and stupid." *Dorothy Parker*

Create First-Date Chemistry

Well you got this far – always a good sign. Now that you're sitting opposite him, it's time to begin making a connection. Naturally, a first date is not the time to talk about your controlling ex or intimacy issues/gas bill/work problems. Keep it light, with plenty of laughter and smiles. The following ideas will maintain his interest.

- Be jokey. That doesn't mean leaning back in your chair and guffawing loudly at your own jokes. The art of chit-chat is to sprinkle your conversation with light, fun anecdotes. Say something amusing about the journey over or make a humorous observation about a topical subject.

- Tease him a bit. It shows you have a sense of humour and will help you both relax. But don't go over-the-top and poke fun at his quiff/Mohican or baggy trousers: he'll either be irritated or hurt by this.

- Tell a funny story with some gentle innuendo, not too much or you might look like you are up for it, but just enough to titillate his juices. It will create sexual chemistry.

- Introduce a gentle tug of war to get the sexual chemistry going. Every now and then, disagree with what he says. It will make him a bit anxious and as soon as you're nice to him again, he will mistake it for attraction.

- Reveal a little leg or cleavage (not both at the same time) while doing all of the above. It shows you are body-confident and playful.

- Disappear at some point – about 10 minutes will do. This will give him time to miss you.

- Mix up the messages. "Oh, you're so handsome/cool/well dressed," you say, smiling, then turn away and yawn. The more distant you are, the more this engages the emotions. Make him work for your attention.

Chatting Up

The whole point of a first date is to get to know your cub. Do you have things in common, or is it time to pick up the tab and make a quick exit? By the way, you should always pay unless he slaps down his Gold Amex and says it's on him (unlikely unless he's Alpha or Caddish Cub, see pages 59 and 62). The shortest route to interesting table talk is to discover what intrigues the other person. Watch his face: when he lights up, you can proceed with confidence. Here are some first-date topics that will get you bonding.

- "What's your favourite film?" Easy, fun and everyone loves to talk about their favourite movie. Be prepared for generational differences on this one.

- "If you had a million dollars, what would you spend it on?" This is a good way to make your date's eyes light up as he describes his spree.

- "If your house was burning down, what would you save?" You'll learn a good deal about what your date is really like by finding out what he thinks is important to him. Is it an old toy that has sentimental meaning (he's sensitive) or his brand-new iPad (loves novelty)?

- "What's your secret talent?" This is a challenging question and a really good opportunity for your date to show off with impunity. Maybe it's not one to start off with but perhaps toward the end of the date, especially if chemistry is in the air.

- "If you could wake up anywhere in the world tomorrow, where would it be?" Another good question as it gets the imaginative juices flowing and reveals your date's inner values and desires.

- "What do you like to do for fun?" It helps to know if you can share leisure activities. Also, whether he is an outdoor person.

- "What is your favourite band and why?" This is a good opportunity to learn about the latest music and maybe you could introduce him to some of your favourite tunes too.

Seven Deadly Dating Sins

* Remember, a date is a two-way event so don't just talk about yourself. You may be older, more sophisticated and experienced, but asking your boy about himself and his interests will warm him to you.

* Don't judge a boy by his clothes: you can't tell what someone is like just by looking at their personal style, especially a younger man. Baggy trousers and a yellow T-shirt may be the new cool.

* He might not be your type, but don't cut the date short for this reason. If you feel an overwhelming desire to make your excuses and jump in your car, don't be childish. Try to feign an interest when he tells you about his job in sales. Keep smiling and look for a polite time to make your exit. Be gracious: young men have egos, too.

* Avoid digging into his dating past: he may be so young that he hasn't got one. Besides it's only a first date and this will make him feel uncomfortable.

* Don't order complicated, messy food. You'll either end up with spinach on your teeth (we all know that one) or you'll put him off with slurping sounds. What about something fun and light like tapas? This is a great food to share and maybe it will help to break the ice. Check for allergies and veggie boys – it might prove awkward if you book at table at a Mexican steak house!

* Whatever you do, don't use two-for-one vouchers for a first date: it will make you look tight.

* Never bring your baggage to the table. Your ex might be a narcissistic control freak and perhaps you still feel guilty about being bitchy toward your best friend, but keep it to yourself. Too much, too soon is never attractive. A first date is the time to show him your best points.

And finally, don't propose marriage … unless you never want to see him again.

The Generation Gap

During the date there may be times when you feel like you're on another planet. This is normal: remember, you're dating a cute guy from another era. Here are some of the most common generational fear factors.

* You feel like you don't belong. You're talking dinner-party faux pas, he's raving about his PlayStation: suddenly it's as if you're from two different places. Relax, it's only natural: bring him back to you with one of the questions on page 105 or go to the bathroom to take stock and reboot.

* You see a group of kitties giggling at you at the next table (see also pages 86–7). Maybe it's time to up the flirt factor. Take your cub's hand, canoodle and smile like a Cheshire cat. Show those minxes you're not embarrassed to be out with a younger man.

* You catch sight of your reflexion in the mirror: "Omigod!" you shriek. Suddenly you feel like a wrinklie old auntie. Don't worry: it's just a twinge of Older Woman Syndrome (OWS). Go and apply some lipgloss and remember he's on a date with you because he likes you.

Time to Dump Your Date When ...

* He's rude to the barman and/or waiter.

* All his time is spent ogling other women in the restaurant.

* Sticking needles in your eyes would be light relief – he's *sooo* dull!

* He starts talking about his ex.

* Half the date is lost with him twittering and/or texting on his BlackBerry.

* He makes it obvious that he's only with you because he had nothing else to do that night.

* He's only after your money and doesn't want to get to know you.

* You recognize him – and suddenly remember you dated his father!

To Kiss or Not to Kiss?

So, you had a fabulous first date. It turns out you both love James Bond movies and share a mutual loathing for peanut butter. Whether you lean in politely and go for the mwah, mwah social kiss or engage in a round of deep-throat tonsil hockey, follow these kissing rules and you'll soon be smooching with confidence.

* Having pieces of spinach (or for that matter, any other food debris) wedged between your molars and encircled by cracked lips won't do you any favours. Before you leave the bar/restaurant, check your smooch status. Reapply your lipgloss and freshen up.

- If you think your breath might be a bit smelly, don't get paranoid. To check if you have bad breath, lick the back of your hand and sniff. Use a mouthwash before you go out and carry peppermints or freshener spray around with you. Don't let your cub run away in dismay. If he legs it, it's time to pay a visit to the dentist!

- Crinkle factor: Lips like crinkly cardboard are unlikely to make you kissable. Yet chapped lips often happen and are caused by you inhaling through your mouth rather than your nose. There are lots of lip balms on the market that will make you pucker perfect. Similarly, you can brush away dry skin with a toothbrush.

- Don't go OTT with lipgloss, though. Often this can have a gooey effect.

"The worst thing a man can do is kiss me on the first date."
Halle Berry

Go, Girl!

As you stand facing him, give him the green light by saying how much you enjoyed the date. Touch his arm slowly and keep smiling. If he doesn't take the hint and looks as if he's about to cry, don't force it: a gentle peck-hug combo is in order. Otherwise, a soft, slow kiss that grazes the cheek is a good way to ease into a full-on kissing marathon. The rest is up to you. Whether you play it cool and leave him waiting for more or make him breakfast the following morning, a good date will end with a text from him and the promise of more to come.

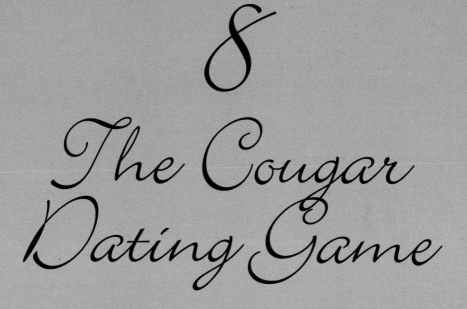

8
The Cougar Dating Game

"When you're young, your whole life is about the pursuit of fun. Then you grow up and learn to be cautious. You could break a bone or a heart. You look before you leap and sometimes you don't leap at all because there's not always someone there to catch you. And in life, there's no safety net. When did it stop being fun and start being scary?"

Sarah Jessica Parker (Carrie in *Sex and the City*)

It's a Cougar World

OK, the first date went well and you can't wait to see him again. All you can think about is his goofy smile and mop of curly hair when he watches *Scooby-Do* reruns. You may be in lust for him and why shouldn't you be? But try to take things slowly. Don't drop everything – your friends/work/gym/cocktail parties – and rush over to his flat to eat baked beans out of a can and watch YouTube. After all, it's early days and you may be setting yourself up for a fall.

Know What You Want

Use your cat-like skills to figure out what you want from your cub. Before you start dating, think about your relationship expectations. Maybe casual is more your speed and seeing him less frequently will not be a problem. And after years of a serious relationship or marriage, dating for fun with no-strings attached could be just what you need. But if there is an expectation of a serious relationship, then seek out a younger man who is looking for the same: don't be afraid to voice what you want. Being on the same page at the beginning will prevent frustration and heartbreak later on if you then discover he doesn't want the same thing. Here's how to handle it.

If you want to keep it casual, lighthearted and no-strings: Don't talk about the future or meeting his parents and friends.

You want to cuddle and look after your cub back at your lair: Give him your card and let him do the follow-up.

You're not sure: Keep your options open and date other younger guys to figure out if he's the one you want. This prevents you from getting emotionally attached too soon.

"You're seeing a lot of younger men with older women and it's because there are no defined rules of engagement. Anything goes socially ... women in their 30s and 40s are open to dating men in their 20s."

Jodi DeLuca

Stop Gap or Start?

Many women choose to become cougars because they're not interested in long-term commitment and enjoy the short-term pleasure and fabulous sex that dating a hot young himbo gives.

You're in it for the short term if ...

* You're so busy with your career that you don't have time to get involved in another serious relationship.

* Maybe you've been married and you're tired of doing all the giving/work in return for so little.

* Or you love being a single, modern woman.

* Perhaps you want pleasurable company for now.

* Or, you just want to fill the sex gap.

You're in it for the long term if ...

* You often feel lonely and find yourself watching the Discovery Channel at 3 am.

* You miss him when he's gone.

* You're keen to introduce him to your close friends and family.

* You've been hurt by old codgers and are feeling raw.

* You just can't stop thinking about him. You're in love!

Let Him Be the Guy

Despite being a younger man, he is *still* a man. He likes the hunt and the chase, so let him take the lead in asking you for your phone number and the first date. His pursuit will prove that he really is into you.

Pay Attention

Remember, he's only young and even if he is buying you dinner and sending you bunches of roses, underneath all that youthful bravado he may be nervous. Every now and then, give him some encouragement by showing him how much you like him.

- Get to know his favourite bands and burn a compilation CD.

- Take him away for a weekend at an elegant hotel.

- Order up his favourite films and watch them together.

- Try hard to fit in/get on with his friends/sister/other family members.

- Within reason, let him play video games when he comes over.

Be Proud of Your Cub!

When taking your date out for a bite to eat or buying clothes (well, you always hated that Abercrombie hoodie) or while holding hands/kissing in the back row of the cinema, you're bound to run into someone you know at some stage. Here's what to do.

Don't blush and pretend he's your nephew. For a start, this may hurt the person you care about (the under-25s have feelings as well). More importantly, it will show that you're not comfortable with dating someone outside your age group.

Do keep the conversation light. Introduce your cub and let your boss/ex sister-in-law/son's teacher know that you value your companion (even if he's shuffling from foot to foot like startled prey).

Don't Get Sappy, Stay Savvy

Younger men often find it very appealing to be with a woman who doesn't need constant reassurance about how she looks, or doesn't require them to stroke a fragile ego. A top cougar will *never* say …

* Does my bum look big in this?

* Where is this going?

* Do you love me?

A classy cougar *will* say …

🐾 Mine's a double Martini on the rocks – shaken and stirred!

🐾 Hey, I've just picked up your scent and I like it.

🐾 Grrrr, let me take you home and stroke your fur!

"I've dated men my age, younger than me and older. The only difference is the young ones are quicker at taking out the garbage."
Lara Flynn Boyle

Keep a Sense of Humour
(While Showing Off Your Experience)

A lot of younger men are drawn to older women because of their sexual expertise and the promise of what they have to offer between the sheets. True cougars ...

- Are enthusiastic and not scared to initiate the show. What else would the handcuffs be for?

- Keep the refrigerator well stocked with champagne, strawberries and chilled massage oil.

- Know the power of showing how much they enjoy the pleasures of their prey. Acting coy is for the younger kitten.

- Have watched *The Graduate* 20 times – well, at least the seduction scene. After all, Mrs Robinson is every young man's adolescent fantasy.

- Are proud of their bodies and keep the light on.

- Never reveal their age, especially during a moment of passion. He'll have an immediate picture of his grey-haired, ageing aunt and no amount of sex toys will get his desire back.

- Are ready for Round Three and Four. A cougar is well aware that sex is stimulating, great for the abs and keeps her skin looking fresh.

"Attraction is not a choice."

David DeAngelo

In Love or In Lust?

OK, so everything is going swimmingly but after a few weeks, it's useful to review the situation. You may now be planning the honeymoon, while he could be looking for a bit of a change. Just because you think you have more chemistry than a science lab doesn't mean you are in love. Consider the following.

He's in love when ...

* He introduces you to his parents.

* Or makes plans for Christmas and it's only February.

* It's important to him that you get on with his childhood friends.

* He decides to decorate his flat just the way you like it.

* He begs you to go to the fertility clinic.

He's only in it for a good time when ...

* At weekends, he's always busy.

* He only phones/texts to come over late at night.

* Often he cancels plans at the last minute to go rollerblading with his mates.

* He's not interested in meeting your friends.

* You sometimes catch him ogling young kittens.

Toy Boy Wooing

(Bridging the Age Gap)

So there you are snuggled under the duvet, eating chocolate ice-cream, or chasing each other round the bedroom. He's fun and you love being in his company. The trouble is that when he's with his friends, he burps at will, says things like,"Hey, dude" and rushes off to have a water fight. Suddenly those bulging biceps and smooth skin don't make up for the fact that you're dating an adolescent guy. Here's what to do.

Pick and choose the events you go to with him. Some evenings – an all-night rave with warm beer and a night in a soggy tent – only highlight the fact that your tastes are wildly different.

Don't force yourself on his world. If you don't find the newest craze on YouTube funny, then don't laugh: his friends will be able to tell you're faking it. Be yourself, ask questions and get them to talk about it – they'll be flattered by your interest.

Spend evenings apart. Tired of playing "tackle" in bed? Attend that lecture on Middle Eastern art/chick-flick with your friends and let him do his own thing.

Find things you both like. Maybe you share an interest in horror films, Chinese food or long walks in the countryside. It's a great opportunity to bond.

Boy Talk

To help you communicate better with your boy, here are 10 of the most popular texting acronyms that he will definitely use:

BTW – By the Way	CTN – Can't Talk Now
IDC – I Don't Care	ILY – I Love You
JW – Just Wondering	SRY – Sorry
YTB – You're The Best	GF – Girl Friend
L8R – Later	CBL – Come Back Later

The Black Tie Event

So you buy him his first tuxedo and take him along to that work do/charity event/ wedding. He may look like he's just stepped off the catwalk, but inside he could be feeling as stiff as a piece of cardboard. To help you decide whether or not you want to include him, here are some considerations.

Is it worth it? Will attending your daughter's wedding make him/you feel so uncomfortable that you end up having to do a damage limitation exercise by peeling him off the floor when he gets drunk on the free champagne?

Is he only doing it to please you? If he has any reservations at all about standing around with lots of forty-something bankers/real estate managers or even your old relatives, let him stay at home. Give him the run of the house and ask him to wait up for you with a chilled glass of champagne. Or see him some other time.

Make sure he will fit in. A cougar doesn't worry what the world thinks, but she does care about keeping her cub happy. If you're in any doubt about him fitting in, ring the hostess first and check the type and age of guest.

Pitfalls of Cougar Dating

The times they may be changing when it comes to women and younger men, but like anything else in life, there are still pitfalls to look out for when it comes to dealing with a younger man.

- ✳ He has a high sex drive and may not want to be exclusive.

- ✳ His credit ratings could be low and he'll expect you to pay for everything.

- ✳ He's young enough to be your son.

- ✳ He loves your kids and one day he wants some of his own.

- ✳ His mother thinks you are the Devil in Chanel.

- ✳ He's obviously resentful of your career/money and *savoir faire.*

"I can't go on any more bad dates. I would rather be home alone than out with some guy who sells socks on the Internet!"

Cynthia Nixon **(Miranda Hobbs in *Sex and the City*)**

Beware the Cougar Traps

The dating jungle is full of minefields and if there's one thing that's guaranteed to get you a bad reputation, it's being the Oldest Swinger in Town. It may be tempting to try and hold back the years, but clothes should make us look more attractive than we are naked, not less. Besides, wanting to look 15 years younger than your actual age smacks ever so slightly of desperation. Here are some looks that anyone over 30 should avoid.

1661 syndrome. Whereby a woman looks like a bouncy-haired, pert-bottomed kitty from behind and a grandmother from the front. Not only will you look like you're trying far too hard, this could also give him the impression that you're not really comfortable with who you are.

Being fashion roadkill. This includes squeezing into bandage minidresses or micro shorts (only designed for size zeros), wearing leopard-print stretch dresses and too much make-up. Ditto skimpy jeans: the body may be able to take it, but again trying to be a Cheryl Cole look-alike will only make you appear older.

Trying to look like your daughter. Just don't do it!

Having too much flesh on display. Bare midriffs (even if you're flat as an ironing board): no, no, no! Flimsy camisoles with splodgy bat wings are a worse crime – even if you do practise yoga every day, you're not Britney Spears. Baring your shoulders, back and collarbone is far more sophisticated.

"Save a boyfriend for a rainy day – and another, in case it doesn't rain."
Mae West

What to Avoid When Dating a Younger Guy

To help you through what might otherwise be a steep learning curve, here's what to steer clear of when dating a toy boy.

Don't share your sexual history. Being with a younger man is all about the here and now. Why dredge up your past husbands/lovers? It might sound fun slagging off the ex, but your boy's bound to compare his performance/status/kudos and he could come off feeling short.

Too much information (TMI). It may seem like love – you talk all night, laugh and play – but that doesn't mean you have to share too much of your past life. He doesn't need to know the details of your hysterectomy/mother's illness. Keep it light!

Showing off about your career. Chances are, he's on the first or second rung of the ladder at the bank/film company (or even an unpaid intern). The last thing he needs is for you to make him feel like a loser by going on about how you just made partner, blah, blah, blah …

Taking too much control. You may have been in charge of your life/career for a long time now but that doesn't mean you have to grab the wine list every time you enter a restaurant, or buy the cinema/theatre tickets. Don't treat him like a child and boss him around. Let him organize your trip to Belize or get the cinema tickets – all men, even young ones, want to feel useful.

Being a sugar mama. You may want to pick him up and cuddle him all the time, but resist smothering him with affection/gifts/holidays/paying the rent. You're coming on too strong and he'll sense it and either run away, or hang around your house like a bad smell.

The Dating Doubt

This dating malarkey is a new thing for both of you and sometimes you may get the toy-boy heebie-jeebies. Often it can strike when he's been with his friends/ on Facebook/listening to his favourite bands: suddenly you feel the yawning age chasm open up. Just stop and consider carefully: he's out with *you* because he likes who *you* are, how *you* look and what *you* bring to the relationship. Accept it and move on.

So, Is He a Cad or a Cub for Keeps?

You may be dating and doting on him, but how can you tell if the boy sharing your noodles (and your bed) is a cad or a keeper? Try our fun quiz and find out for yourself. Select whether you agree/disagree with each of the questions and then count up your total number of As and Bs.

1 Do you and your toy boy share the same taste in music?
Agree **A**   Disagree **B**

2 Ever find yourself getting bored in his company?
Agree **B**   Disagree **A**

3 Does he offer to pay for little things?
Agree **A**   Disagree **B**

4 Do you laugh at the same jokes?
Agree **A**   Disagree **B**

5 Does he make you feel cherished and content?
Agree **A**   Disagree **B**

6 Has he ever ignored you when you're with your friends?
Agree **B**   Disagree **A**

7 Does your cub often compliment you on how you look?
Agree **A**   Disagree **B**

8 Do you go out in the daytime with him?
Agree **A**   Disagree **B**

9 Does he seem more in love with your body than your mind?
Agree **B**   Disagree **A**

10 Does he often take you to family functions?
Agree **A**   Disagree **B**

11 Do you feel embarrassed to be seen with your cub in public?
Agree **B**   Disagree **A**

12 Does your boy think you're the hottest mama since Madonna?
Agree **A**   Disagree **B**

13 Does he share his hopes and fears with you?
Agree **A**   Disagree **B**

14 When you're out, does your cub open doors/get you a cab?
Agree **A**   Disagree **B**

15 Does he make fun of your musical/film tastes?
Agree **B**   Disagree **A**

Cub for Keeps (between 12 and 15 As)
Your cub is trying hard to impress you. He loves the way you look and hangs onto your every word. You both seem to have a lot of things in common. Be careful: he could fall hard and may end up getting hurt if you're not on the same wavelength.

He Could Be Worth It (between 9 and 12 As)
You have things in common and he pushes some of your buttons, but it's early days and this one is on a learning curve. Maybe it's worth sticking with this a while longer and teaching him a few courtship moves that you particularly like.

Friend With Benefits (between 5 and 9 As)
He's a good guy and you like each other, but you have to ask yourself: is this what you're looking for? This one is great for a few dates and a roll in the hay. But if you're looking for a more satisfying relationship, he's way too immature.

Dump Him Now! (between 0 and 4 As)
This one is a struggle. Now there's no point excusing his caddish behaviour just because he's young. If he wanted a sincere relationship (for however long), then he would be willing to change. Some men are just plain selfish. End of story.

9
Great
Sexpectations

"Is sex dirty? Only if it's done right!"

Woody Allen

OK, so you've snared your hot young prey, shared a few wonderful dates and now you're both dying to rip each other's clothes off. Time to take it to the bedroom.

Feline Fear

No matter how confident a cougar you might be, when it comes to baring all you're bound to experience moments of pre-pounce panic. Questions such as "Have I aged rapidly?", "Omigod! Is that cellulite or a relief map on my thighs?" or even "Is that my bottom or porridge in a string bag?" may hurtle through your mind at the speed of a freight train. Relax. For a start when a man (especially a young one) thinks sex is on the horizon, he's not thinking about how large your thighs/stomach are, he's more likely to have his tongue hanging out and be ready to ravage you.

> **"Kinky is using a feather. Perversion is using the whole chicken."**
>
> *Unknown*

Sexy Secrets

Feeling sexy is a way of thinking. The following hot tips will help to increase your self-awareness and self-confidence and get you pounce-prepared.

I think I'm sexy, I feel I'm sexy ... To be sexy, don't carry your feline fears into the bedroom. Try not to think, "God, I'm soooo flabby/wrinkly/fat" when your toy boy is kissing your thighs/neck/stomach. To boost body confidence, give yourself a reality check. Next time you're at the store or in the gym/park, take a look around you at all the attractive women who are a variety of shapes and sizes. Now conjure up a sexy image of yourself and remember that great sex begins in the head!

Walk with va-va-voom. The next time you're strolling down the street, slow your pace and see how your body moves. Let your hips sway slightly from side to side and start thinking dirty thoughts. Take note of the movement of your hips and the expression on your face. Be careful: you may soon be stopping traffic.

Get yourself a goodie box. Yes, yes, yes! Sex toys. From the Rampant Rabbit (a vibrator with six stimo-settings – the trouble is, it's so good, you may never go back to the real thing) to furry handcuffs, fruity lubes or feathers, props are fun. They help to loosen any inhibitions and will liven up your bedroom. Think Miranda in *Sex and the City*: she had a whole goodie drawer ready to turn herself and her man into quivering wrecks.

Wear sexy underwear. Whatever you wear now, bump it up a notch. Buy something sensuous and naughty, a garment you would never consider wearing and wear it under your everyday clothes. No one needs to know but you and you'll feel super-sexy keeping the secret!

Bathing beauty. Light some aromatherapy candles and run a warm, sensual bath. Sprinkle a few drops of lavender, jasmine or patchouli oil on the water's surface to feel sexy and bold. Lie back and luxuriate. You can spray linen with your favourite scent too.

Mirror, Mirror. Place mirrors around your room so you can see your reflection in the glass. Men get turned on visually and the sight of you licking him like a lollipop will get him firmly in the moan zone.

Bring out your inner Dita Von Teese: Buy a DVD of the famous burlesque dancer and imitate her moves. Put on some sexy music and bump and grind until you feel hot to trot. Close your eyes and let yourself go. Think sexy thoughts and you'll soon be revved up.

"I dig skin, lips and Latin men." *Madonna*

Sexy Cougar Skills

There he is, your adorable Adonis is lying unclothed on the bed. And just the sight of you is enough to give any young man an erection. Naturally, you may be a little nervous. If so, you might feel better if you undress slowly and sexily. The trick is not to pounce too soon or it will all be over in a matter of seconds. But any cougar worth her salt knows exactly what to do with that precious stick of dynamite she has in her sights. So take the lead and he'll love you for it. Try these tricks to get the ball rolling and let him know just how sexy a cougar can be.

Stroke his ego. Before you get down to flipping his switch, a little flattery will make him feel relaxed and open. Men worry that they are not big/potent enough. When a woman says, "Ooooh, it's *soooo* big/hard," it's a bit like a man saying, "You are the prettiest woman I've met." Really!

Below the belt. Now that you're both relaxed and comfortable, tease to please. Run your fingertips along his thigh, caress lightly, press firmly and tickle gently. Teasing him will hit his pleasure zone and he'll soon be begging you to get on down! Be careful: if he is very young or a virgin, you may have to slow things down to curb his excitement.

Flip his switch. Time to connect with the instrument itself. Love it, adore it, you can never pay too much attention to "Mr Happy". If you really want to make him grip the sheets, stroke the head of his penis/rim around the bottom of the head and the long ridge running the length of the underside – these are his hot spots.

Anyone for tennis? Did you know that while gently does it for a woman, men prefer a firm grip when it comes to getting hold of their manhood? So hold his penis as if it's a tennis racket and get ready to serve.

Stroke of genius. Stroke his gristle missile firmly, smoothly and in a steady rhythm and you'll soon have him in the moan zone. If you spot that he's about to do a rendition of a volcano, remove your hand gently and smoothly. Stop the action. Get a glass or two of champagne from the refrigerator and take a breather. Let him know that a clever cougar is in control of the game.

Give me some flour. Kneed his penis between both hands as if it's a piece of dough. Roll it between palms and stroke the underside with the palm of one hand. Roll or thump it against your belly, thigh or face. That thing is yours to do with as you will and I guarantee he'll love every sexy second of it.

Tongue twister. If there's one thing that separates the cougars from the kitties, it's oral sex. A cougar knows that a penis is never happier than when in her mouth. Treat it as if it's the tastiest lollipop to keep your cub coming back for more. Send a jolt of erotic electricity by licking the head of his penis and then suck on it like a piece of hard candy. Yum!

Ball boy. A lot of men love having their balls played with but are far too shy to ask a woman to do this. Take them one at a time in your mouth, gently lick his testicles and act as if you are his sexual slave. It will make him feel special (again, it's like him buying you a romantic present).

No more honey in the jar. If you really want to have naughty fun, then dip his penis into a jar of honey, jam or maple syrup and lap it up. Be careful of the calories – if he loves this little trick, you could find yourself turning into tubby cougar.

"An erection is like the Theory of Relativity – the more you think about it, the harder it gets." *Unknown*

Mastering the Main Course

By now the action will have hotted up nicely. Now it's time to lie back and really get him into you. For happy horizontal hoopla, lying there motionless while he pumps up and down and then rolls over in a sweaty heap is for inexperienced kitties and old codgers. Great sex is an art. Here is the ultimate guide to some of the best body rattlers to keep you in pole position.

Missionary Magic: Lying back is probably the safest, most intimate position of all and it's great to start off with. Give things a boost by raising your legs so that your knees are pressed to your chest. The higher you go, the deeper he can thrust. Push him into you with each stroke and gyrate those hips. Go for it, girl!

Woman on Top: Getting on top takes a cougar-like skill. Slide slowly into position and gyrate your hips in slow motion. This position is good for caressing and intimacy, but beware the "forward droop". As you lean forward, everything sags and bags (check in the mirror alone to see if this is a good look for you). Otherwise, give him the Turnaround. Mount him the other way, facing away from him. Not only will this hide any sagging and bagging, but your butt looks good and firm. Jiggle up and down and ride him like a horse.

Spooning: This is the perfect canoodling position (great for early morning, lazy love-making). Lie on your side away from him so that he enters you from behind, with his arms wrapped round you.

Doing the Dog: The ultimate deep penetration, this one is the rock and roll of sex. Get on all fours so he enters you from behind. This one pushes all his buttons: he can see your cute derrière (which incidentally looks firm and slim in this position) and he'll feel like a powerful predator taking you. You can also do this one lying down. Put a pillow (or two) under your hips – for a better view and deeper penetration – and push back into him.

Getting Jiggy With It

A cougar may be accustomed to sex with her ex hubbie/lover (more antique than sexual antics), followed by the inevitable post-coital roll-over and snore. Sex with the younger man is a completely different experience. Here's what you can look forward to.

- A young man will reboot in five minutes and go again for hours; he has more go in him than a Duracell battery!

- With all the flexibility of a gymnast and the strength of a body builder, your boy will fling you round the bed like Gungha Din and have more raunch than Rambo.

- More than likely he'll pounce on you in the kitchen, in office, at some smart event. After all, he has the time, energy and sheer *joie de vivre*, unlike a clapped-out codger.

- He won't be scared to ask what it takes to ensure you have an earth-shattering orgasm.

- Or roll over and let you sleep in the wet patch.

- And after mind-blowing sex, he could even become completely besotted with you.

"Sex is a part of nature: I go along with nature." *Marilyn Monroe*

Anytime, Any Place, Anywhere

Take your love trysts outdoors to spice things up even further. The risk of being spotted will up the heat factor and provide an added frisson. Whatever you do, be discreet and don't go where there might be children. Location, location … Here are some ideas to get you started.

In the park: Wear a long skirt without underwear. Find a secluded park bench, subtly lift your skirt and sit on top of him (he should wear easy-access trousers). You won't need to wriggle long to get a result.

On the grass: Take the missionary outdoors. Again, a floaty skirt is advisable as is a big blanket to cover you up.

Engine Trouble: If you get excited while driving down the motorway, pull over into a secluded spot. Lock the doors and climb onto his lap. Face away from him with your feet on the floor for maximum penetration. But be careful: you don't want naughty neighbours looking in.

In the public lavatory: Whether you're at the office/museum/department store, giving him a knee-trembling blow job (or vice versa) is enough to rev up anyone's raunch. Be sure to find a cubicle that is big enough, well kept and sweet smelling. For added oomph, try straddling him on the loo seat and get ready for the ride of your lives.

"It's impolite to have sex anywhere that is visible to other people who aren't having sex." *Jenny Eclair*

Pleasure Pitfalls

When it comes to bediquette, there are some things a clever cougar should avoid. Never, ever …

Call round when you're drunk and beg for sex. "Shaalloo, it's meeee," you say, ringing his doorbell at two in the morning, with breath like a sewer and mascara running down your cheeks. The drunken bootie call is such a no-no for any sophisticated cougar.

Ask if it's in yet. If he's more mini dong than King Kong, you will have given him a complex for life.

Say it's a wee bit tiny. At best you'll scar him for life and you could even turn him into a complete misogynist.

Ask if it was OK. It's a bit like him saying you're an OK-looking bird.

Say your ex was better. Seems obvious, but it does happen.

Bark orders. "Up a bit, left a bit, down a bit … No, you fool, that's my belly button!" Be patient, take his hand and guide him, all the while telling him how good he is.

> **"Sex is like good Bridge. If you don't have a good partner, you'd better have a good hand."** *Mae West*

What Flips Your Switch?

Are you an untamed Alley Cat smelling of sweat and sex, or a Perfect Pussy looking for romance? When it comes to sex, we all have a different persona. Discover what flips your switch with our fun quiz. Study the following statements and in each case, pick the one that suits you best.

1 Sex with a new toy boy is ...
   a) The most exciting part so long as you're the one in control.
   b) Exhilarating and erotic, you love the thrill of the new.
   c) A bit nerve-wracking – you prefer it when you've got to know each other a bit better.

2 Which of the following fantasies appeals to you most?
   a) You, your partner, a whip and some melted chocolate.
   b) Role-play situations involving you and your cub.
   c) A weekend holed up in a romantic hotel with champagne and fluffy towels.

3 How do you feel about being naked in front of your boy?
   a) I don't think about it at all. He's lucky to be with me.
   b) I accept my sags and bags, and hope my personality shines through.
   c) I keep the lights down low until I know he really fancies me.

4 Which one of these would get you in the mood?
   a) Delicious finger food, champagne and a luxury hotel room.
   b) An exciting conversation or a daring sexual approach.
   c) A kiss and a cuddle.

5 Experimenting with new positions and ways to make love is ...
   a) What it's all about.
   b) OK, so long as you don't have the Kama Sutra in your hand.
   c) It's important, but I prefer to connect in an emotional way.

6 What's your preferred sexual position?
   a) On top, so I'm in control.
   b) Doggy style – it's sexy and a bit naughty.
   c) Missionary: I love the intimacy and gazing face-to-face.

7 What do you wear in the bedroom?
   a) Stocking, suspenders and a black corset.
   b) Edible underwear – it's fun and playful.
   c) A cute satin Teddy.

8 What pleases you most?
   a) A 69 – what else?
   b) Sex toys.
   c) Making passionate love.

9 What's your sexual style?
   a) Lots of scratching and biting.
   b) Playful throws and laughter.
   c) Sweet, slow and tender.

10 You are most attracted to your cub because …
   a) He's toned, honed and handsome.
   b) Something about him gives you the goose bumps.
   c) Whenever you see him, your heart skips a beat.

Mostly As
Top Cat
You like to take the lead when it comes to the bedroom. In fact, being in control is what turns you on. You're the perfect cat for a cub in training and he'll feel safe and secure for you know exactly what you're doing. Be careful you don't turn into a bedroom bully and start barking orders at him like a sergeant major, though!

Mostly Bs
Alley Cat
Vibrant and erotic, you love to take sexual risks to rev things up a bit. There's no doubt that when it comes to play, you're an exciting and fun cat to be with. Be careful that you don't lose sight of your emotions, though: using sex to cover up for intimacy issues is not healthy.

Mostly Cs
Perfect Pussy
The most romantic of all the cats, you want to feel special and loved for exactly who you are. That may be worthy, but be careful not to tone down that vital oomph factor. Work in a bit of naughty stuff to keep the tempo hot – you're sexier than you think!

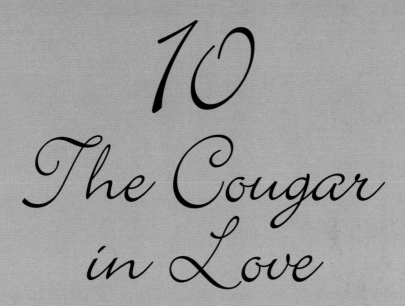

10
The Cougar
in Love

"Soul-mates are people who bring out the best in you. They are

not perfect but are always perfect for you."

Unknown

The "luurve" word may not have been unleashed as yet,

but if you are still seeing each other after a few months (he

has his own drawer at your place and you have got over

the fact that he was three when you were at college) then

congratulations: you are officially now a couple!

After all, even the most glamorous and carefree cougar can fall for her cub. One day you are shagging the hot young gardener, the next he is planting your favourite flower and naming it after you. Maybe you are entertaining thoughts of him moving in/buying a 50-inch plasma TV/being exclusive. Before you give him the key to your condo and to your heart, here are a few pointers to tell if you are on the Love Train.

- You are desperate to introduce him to your entire family/children/ closest friends.

- You are prepared to drive miles to see his favourite band.

- Whenever he is not there, you think about him.

- You find yourself thinking about the future and he is in it.

- You are insanely jealous when he talks to young kitties (you don't show it, of course).

- You get stressed out if he goes on holiday with his mates.

- You want to be exclusive.

- You've stopped treating him like your pet.

- You both laugh/get bored at the same bits in movies.

- You listen to his boy stories even though you have matchsticks keeping your eyes open.

But it's time to get off at the next stop if …:

- You object to him feeling too much at home in your apartment.

- He irritates you if he hangs around at the weekend.

- You instinctively keep him away from your family/children and friends.

* You want to cop off with his friends.

* You don't laugh at his jokes anymore.

* His youth-lingo ("I've got a wedgie") is so irritating you have taken to wearing earplugs.

* You are always grumpy and niggling him.

* You realize the young adorable cub you once dated really wants a mother substitute.

* He just wants to spend your money.

* You can't be bothered to drive out of your way to meet him.

The Cougar Effect

While dating younger men might be a great idea and something more and more women are seeing the benefits of, the world still can't get to grips with accepting the old broad/young buck relationship, especially if it becomes serious. It's the old double standard in neon lights with bells on! Wrinkly old septuagenarians trying to cop off with or marrying 21-year-olds is perfectly natural but when it comes to a 45-year-old woman stepping out with or marrying a hot young stripling, you can almost hear the cries of "off with her head!". Not that a confident cougar cares what others think, it's just that if you have decided to "go steady" with your cub, then it's good to be well-prepared for a few attacks that will more than likely come your way.

"You know, lovers really should have a minimum isolation period of say, six months, so as not to nauseate absolutely everyone they meet."

Kathy Lette

How to Survive an Old Codger Attack

Old codgers can get rather nasty when they find themselves confronted with a sassy cougar and her doting cub. After all, you have turned the tables and ditched them in favour of youngsters more than half their age. Here are some things they might do.

An old codger will ...

* Say, "Your son looks nothing like you" and smirk

* Look him up and down and ask if it's a school night.

* Direct all his conversation to you and edge your toy boy out of the way.

* Say, "Shouldn't he be drinking lemonade?", as he knocks back a double scotch on the rocks.

His Friends and Your Friends

It's not only codgers who are resentful of your new-found sex glow. There will be non-cougars out there with their claws out. They may think you're foolish, having a mid-life crisis, and need to wake up and get a reality check.

Some women will ...

* Strike you off their dinner-party list as soon as they clap eyes on your 25-year-old jailbait. It's all too weird!

* Smile at you condescendingly and tell you "It's your money he's after."

* Inform you that your money's better spent on a face-lift.

* Give you the address for SugarMommy.com.

* Ask when you will be reaching the Big 50.

* Say, "So how are you related to this young man?"

His friends will ...

* Ask if you have any hot mommas for them.

* Ask him what it's like to bed an old broad.

* Congratulate and high-five him.

* Get him drunk and introduce him to hot young kittens.

* Remind him constantly of the yawning age gap.

* Think you are vulture-like seductress who eats young prey for breakfast and then try and shag you.

Zip Your Lip

Ok, so you are having the best sex ever! But there's no need to go on and on about it to your female friends. Chances are they are stuck in a "once-a-week-get-your-leg-over" relationship and the last thing they need is your rip-roaring antics shoved in their faces. Spare them the details unless they beg you.

Let Them Come to You

So your friends have struck you off the dinner party/book reading/lunch list and you are stuck in Social Siberia. Fine. Don't go begging to get back in. After all, you have done nothing wrong. Let them know what fun you are having. Have your own parties/lunches and they will soon come to you.

"Little kindness and courtesies are so important in relationships, the little things are the big things." *Stephen R. Covey*

Build a Love Bubble

If you are new to the game, you will need to protect yourself and your cub from some of the catty barbs and codgy innuendo that could be rushing headlong in your direction. Here are a few hints to protect your relationship:

Bulletproof your bond. Spend lots of "us" time – it doesn't have to be glamorous parties/dinners, just time when you focus on each other and your needs and desires. This will strengthen your attachment to each other.

Put your cub first. It doesn't mean you have to give up your life, just that you are actively thinking of your partner's needs and the needs of your relationship. You have decided to be serious, after all.

Listen with your heart and mind. When you are with your cub, listen intently to what he has to say and respect it.

Be firm. If your friends or family attack your cub or your relationship, respond quickly to let them know you will not tolerate such behaviour … and go off for a dirty weekend just to show them!

"It is the things in common that make relationships enjoyable,

but it is the little differences that make them interesting."

Todd Ruthman

Cub Maintenance

How to Stay in the Luurve Zone

So you've reached stage two – somewhere between the 6- and 18-month mark. You are happily in the "I don't have to pretend I like Beavis and Butt Head" stage, you've stopped holding in your stomach every time he comes into view and you both have a "side" of the bed. You've have been grocery shopping together and he even knows your favourite brand of olive oil, real life has kicked in. Well, you can't exist in the "honeymoon period" indefinitely, but when reality bites, don't panic. Study the following pointers to keep you in the Love Zone.

Keep the tryometer on full. Just because you've snared your prey that doesn't mean you have to relax and start clipping your toenails in front of him. Keep the feminine mystique going with sexy lingerie and defuzing – it can go a long way in keeping your cub in the sex zone.

Play the "Pussy in Peril" routine every now and then. After all, it must be difficult living with a confident cougar who has the answer to everything. Seek his advice (even if you know the answer) on property/finance/music. Ask him to put up your shelves – in short, make him feel responsible for you and up his man-ometer.

Stop watching your favourite late-night programme. Turn your attention to your cub instead.

Get away from your usual routine. Drive out to the countryside for breakfast at the weekend. Book a sexy afternoon at one of those hotels by the hour: it will keep you in the moan zone.

Watch posh porn. Rent some of those 1970s' soft porn iconic films such as *Emmanuelle 1* and *2* or *The Green Door* and lock the doors.

Schedule in dine-out nights. Romantic meals where you concentrate on each other will help to rekindle that loving feeling. Going commando (no knickers) wouldn't hurt either!

Simple getaways: They say it isn't what we do, but how we feel when we are doing it. Sometimes just a walk by the sea or getting caught in the rain can kick-start intimacy and feel romantic.

Things to Avoid When You Are in the Love Zone

Slobby single behaviour. Such as: wearing baggy, coffee-stained jim-jams and eating fries in bed unless it's with him. Invest in luxurious leisurewear – soft-to-touch pyjamas – yoga pants with T-shirts: they don't have to be outright sexy, just nice girl sexy.

Getting too domestic too soon. Sure cook/clean and go shopping together, but rearranging his sock drawer, playing Mrs Mop every Monday and spring cleaning his entire apartment will simply make you look like a clean freak and no fun whatsoever.

Trying to change him. Just because he's young and malleable doesn't mean you have to stop him wearing his hoodies/jeans/sneakers and force him into chinos and polo shirts. Love him the way he is.

"I told my mother-in-law that my house was her house, and she said, 'Get the hell off my property!'" *Joan Rivers*

Mommie Dearest

One of the hardest things about age-gap relationships has got to be his mother. After all, she expected her darling son to turn up with a nice young girl and start a family, but there he is standing on the doorstep with a glossy-haired 45-year-old glamourpuss. You do the maths.

What she might do ...

* If you are of a similar age, she will see you as her rival and possibly launch a carefully orchestrated mommy attack.

* Introduce him to girls his own age.

* She will want to know all about you and then tell her friends how awful you are.

* Be jealous as you are prettier/more successful than she is.

* Bitch about you to her son when you are not around.

There you are in your slimfit jeans, honey-kissed hair and stilettos and finally you're face to face with Mama-Pitbull. Make no mistake about it, she won't be happy – unless of course you are mega-rich and or famous and can invite her to the Bahamas at Christmas. To help you navigate the waters, here are few things she might say to you when you have "the talk".

What she says: "I just want him to be happy."
What she means: "You are far too old and will never make him happy."

What she says: "My son is very impressionable."
What she means: "You are predatory and want to manipulate and use him."

What she says: "He's still very young."
What she means: "He is far too young to be involved with an old slapper like you and should be going out with girls his own age."

What she says: "I just want him to have a normal life."
What she means: "This is perverse and I do not approve."

What she says: "Aren't you a bit old to be seeing my son."
What she means: "I will fight you to the death, woman.
I do not want this for my son."

How to handle her ...

Sweet talk: Be warm and genuine. Hopefully she will see that you are not some one-night fling but a serious contender.

Create a connection: Let her talk and voice her fears. This will enable you to become more aware of what makes her tick so you can deal with the situation more effectively.

Don't get angry: It may be hard to understand the anxiety and confusion a mother can feel when her son dates an older woman. Be sensitive to her feelings.

Watch out for monster mother: If she starts calling at all hours of the day, weeping down the phone or constantly bitching behind your back, discuss the problem with your cub.

Know where he stands: If he is torn between you and her, but never supports you, then you need to communicate with him on a serious level. Chances are he is a mommy's boy and if he's not standing up for you now, he never will.

> "There is not a game in the world that you can play
> without getting hurt some." *Katharine Hepburn*

Boys Behaving Badly – the Telltale Signs

So, most men leave the lavatory seat up, go on three-day sulkathons and think that the housework does itself. That's fine, but be on the lookout for the bright red flags. Some young men are just rotters through and through. Don't even start to consider your cub as serious boyfriend material if you spot any of these traits.

* He tells you no one has loved you as much as he does.
  He is manipulating you.

* He is rude about other women, your friends, your family. He is a young control freak and he'll make your life a misery.

* You find yourself making excuses for him because he's young. You feel the need to tell friends/family that he's "not always like that" or "he's just a bit young". Don't downplay his bad behaviour. It won't get any better and you are storing up trouble.

* He disappears for a weekend/few days without telling you. Whats more, he lies to you repeatedly and for no reason. He has no respect for you. Be careful: he is just a bad person and there will be trust issues with this one.

* He always has to win. When you argue, he will stop at nothing – including cruel remarks. He is a narcissist and expects to get his own way.

* If you mention bad behaviour, is he willing to make changes to improve the relationship? A man who is unwilling is not making you a priority.

* He snogs/sleeps with another woman. A man who can't keep his zinger in his trousers does not respect you, and never will.

"I'm miserable if I'm not in love and of course, I'm miserable if I am."
Tallulah Bankhead

Dump or Be Dumped

There will come a time in every cougar's life when she has to break up with her toy boy or vice versa. As with any other relationship splits, endings are never easy or fun and often include a lot of pain. Here's a step-by-step guide to getting back into tip-top hunting condition.

Licking Your Wounds

Often the first few days or weeks after being dumped or ending a relationship are often the most difficult. The emotions that kick in can be unpleasant and painful. Chances are, you've been there before so you know that you need to take time out to wrap yourself in cotton wool. That is, until you feel yourself coming out of the dump tunnel. Here are some break-up does and don'ts.

Do return to your lair. This is a time to lick your paws. Stay indoors, watch upbeat movies and invite good female friends (men are useless, unless they are gay) loaded with wine, chocolates and lots of TLC.

Don't ring/text/email him. It may be tempting to hear his familiar voice and "discuss the break-up" but believe me, if he has dumped you, he is already out there looking for new opportunities.

Do whine/complain/cry over the phone to your friends/sisters/cousins for one week only. We all need to get the emotions out of our system. If you carry on for too long though, they may get weary and have to stage an intervention and cut you off cold turkey.

Don't go into dump denial. It's only natural to feel hate/resentment/anger toward your cub. If you don't work through your feelings, you will never feel the relief and sheer joy of coming through the other side.

Do pamper yourself. Even though you are going through a tough time, don't neglect your grooming/exercise regime. Go to the gym/walks/jogging/have a massage: it will make you feel better and post dump, you will be thankful that you have not disintegrated into a flabby sister.

After a Few Weeks

You've shouted, punched the pillow and cried rivers over him. Now it's time to get out of the house and back on the hunt.

- Start sharking with your fellow cougars. There's nothing more invigorating than a new cub or even just a bit of male appreciation.

- Get a new look. Whether it's blonde highlights, an eye job or a new outfit, this will be a great help in getting your cougar confidence back (and reread pages 23–35).

- If he has treated you badly or been unfaithful, cop off with his best friend/dad/brother should you feel like it. There's nothing better to get you over a cad than the sweet taste of revenge.

- Go on an all-inclusive pampertastic holiday. Get back in tiptop condition with one of those exotic spa breaks. You can swim/snorkel/have an affair with the gorgeous young waiter/water-ski instructor and come back tanned, toned and ready for the hunt.

N B Not all OW/YM relationships break up. In fact, many go on to become permanent liaisons. The point is this: whether you want to get jiggy with it/multi-date or get serious, it's entirely up to you. Just remember one thing: love is ageless. Go, cougar!

Resources

Websites

dateacougartips.com
A blog on dating a cougar, which includes the pros and cons of being a cougar, and general information on the lifestyle

gocougar.com
Women: Why shouldn't you date younger men?
Men: Do you prefer the company of an older woman?
The questions are answered on this website!

www.toyboy.com
Dating website to find "lovely lads" or "successful ladies"

www.singlestravelcompany.com
The company's international "cougar cruise" departs from Miami, Florida, for three nights of fun sailing to the Bahamas. It is specifically for younger men and older women, and even includes roommate matching!

www.cougarevents.com
Join the mailing list to get invited to the best cougar parties and cruises in your city! Mostly American events.

www.urbancougar.com
This is an all round site for cougars. The lifestyle, a community forum and the latest news on celebrity cougars!

www.cougarmingle.com
A dating site for cougars and young men. It is free to place a profile.

www.onlinecougardating.com
A dating site for cougars.

www.toyboywarehouse.com
An online dating site for cougars looking for their toyboy!

www.DateACougar.com
Young men put up their profiles on this website for the cougars to hunt.
You can also search in your area.

www.cougardate.co.uk
A casual dating site for cougars.

www.cougarseekingmen.com
A blog with questions and interviews with real life cougars!

Films to View

American Pie (1999)
The cougar in this film is Stifler's mother. Finch, played by Eddie Kaye Thomas,
is the least likely to lose his virginity first, however at a post-prom party he finds
Stifler's mum in the bedroom...

Class (1983)
Jonathan, played by Andrew McCarthy, goes to a prestigious school where he is
given a room to share with the rich and handsome Skip, played by Rob Lowe.
Skip is annoyed with Jonathan's innocence and is determined for him to lose
his virginity. He sends Jonathan to Chicago where he meets Ellen, played by
Jacqueline Bisset. Little does Skip realize, this is his own mother...

The Graduate (1967)
Mrs Robison, played by Anne Bancroft, bosses around Benjamin, played by Dustin
Hoffman, telling him where to go and what to do. He is seduced by her charm.

Harold and Maude (1971)
Maude, played by Ruth Gordon, proves that even at 79 years old you're never
too old to be a cougar! She gives young and suicidal Harold, played by Bud Cort,
reason to live again.

Loverboy (1989)
Randy Bodek, played by Patrick Dempsey, needs extra cash for college. He falls
in to the lucrative business of sleeping with almost every married woman in town
for money. Alex, played by Barbara Carrera, is the cougar who sets everything
n motion and gets Randy the work; she also sleeps with him!

The Rebound (2010)
Catherine Zeta Jones is a recent divorcée of 40 finding a new life in New York City
when she falls in love with her children's 25-year-old babysitter, Aram Finklestein,
played by Justin Bartha.

Sunset Boulevard (1950)
Joe Gillis, a screenwriter played by William Holden, falls for Norma Desmond,
played by Gloria Swanson. Norma is a silent film star and treats Joe well with
her wealthy lifestyle and income.

What's Eating Gilbert Grape (1993)
Mrs Better Carver, played by Mary Steenburgen, has an affair with Gilbert Grape,
played by Johnny Depp. She is a married woman; he is a delivery boy. The best
quote from this film for cougars out there is: "Gilbert. I'll need a delivery later."

White Palace (1990)
James Spader is a 27-year-old widower who falls for a diner waitress called Nora,
played by Susan Sarandon. Nora is 43 years old, which creates difficulties for the
couple...

Television to View

Accidentally on Purpose
This television programme follows Billie, played by Jenna Elfman,
and her pregnancy resulting from the one-night stand with Zack.

The Cougar
A reality show where an older woman chooses a boyfriend from a group
of 20 younger men. The men have to compete to have a relationship with
a 40-year-old woman.

Cougar Town
Starring Courtney Cox, a recently divorced woman decides to make her dating life more exciting by dating younger men. The tag line "40 is the new 20".

Suggested Reading

Cougar: A Guide for Older Women Dating Younger Men,
Valerie Gibson, Key Porter Books Ltd, 2007.

The Cougar Club, Susan McBride, Avon Books, 2010.

Dating the Younger Man: A Complete Guide to Every Woman's Sweetest Indulgence, Cyndi Targosz, Adams Media, 2008.

Older Women, Younger Men: New Options for Love and Romance,
Felicia Brings and Susan Winter, New Horizon Press, 2000.

The Toyboy Diaries, Wendy Salisbury, Old Street, 2007.

Index

Qualitative GIS

Qualitative GIS

A Mixed Methods Approach

EDITED BY

Meghan Cope and Sarah Elwood

Los Angeles | London | New Delhi
Singapore | Washington DC

First published 2009

SAGE Publications Ltd
1 Oliver's Yard
55 City Road
London EC1Y 1SP

SAGE Publications Inc.
2455 Teller Road
Thousand Oaks, California 91320

SAGE Publications India Pvt Ltd
B 1/I 1 Mohan Cooperative Industrial Area
Mathura Road, Post Bag 7
New Delhi 110 044

SAGE Publications Asia-Pacific Pte Ltd
33 Pekin Street #02-01
Far East Square
Singapore 048763

Library of Congress Control Number 2008939920

British Library Cataloguing in Publication data

A catalogue record for this book is available from the British Library

ISBN 978-1-4129-4565-3
ISBN 978-1-4129-4566-0 (pbk)

Typeset by C&M Digitals (P) Ltd, Chennai, India
Printed by in India at Replika Press Pvt Ltd
Printed on paper from sustainable resources